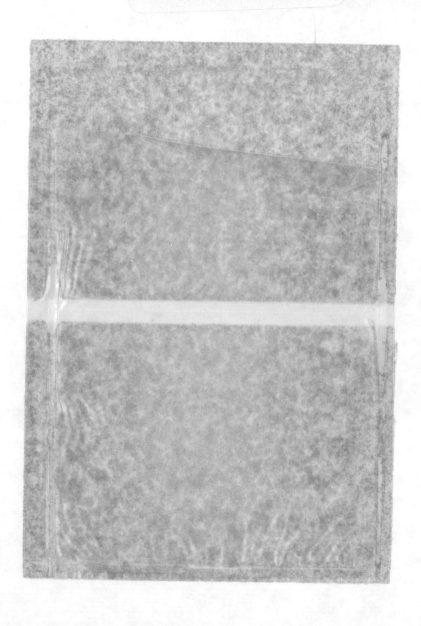

CHRISTIAN INITIATION

IS VOLUME

50

OF THE

Twentieth Century Encyclopedia of Catholicism

UNDER SECTION

V

THE LIFE OF FAITH

IT IS ALSO THE

147TH

VOLUME IN ORDER OF PUBLICATION

Edited by **HENRI DANIEL-ROPS** *of the Académie Française*

CHRISTIAN INITIATION

By *ARTHUR McCORMACK*

HAWTHORN BOOKS · PUBLISHERS · *New York*

First Edition, 1969

CONTENTS

INTRODUCTION

The dictionary defines "initiation" as instruction in first principles.

Initiation is easier to describe than to define, especially with regard to religion. Three important aspects of initiation have been distinguished: (1) the so-called rites of passage which sometimes function as rites of initiation; (2) rites of initiation in the strict sense of the word, i.e., rites introducing people into closed religious societies; (3) initiation in the sense of introduction into the mysteries of religion.

Without pausing now at these technical points, we may describe initiation as a collection of rites and oral teaching by means of which a person experiences a radical change in his religious and social status. As a result of the initiation rites, the neophyte enters into a completely new kind of existence: he becomes a new, a different person. Although not all religions have rites of initiation, every religion does profess to introduce its adherents to eternal truth and divine mysteries. As Dr C. J. Bleeker says, "It is no exaggeration to contend that initiation is one of the key notions of religion, the gate which leads to the knowledge of the nature and of the will of the gods or of the Deity." [1]

This description of initiation, which is applicable to most religions, is especially meaningful when applied to the sacraments of Christian initiation—baptism, confirmation, the Holy Eucharist. By means of these sacraments, a person enters the Christian community; becomes another person, a "new man," a full member of the mystical Body of Christ; passes from death to life; is made partaker of the

---

[1] C. J. Bleeker, ed., *Initiation* (Leiden: E. J. Brill, 1965), p. 15.

mysteries of Christ; is associated with the unique society, the Church of Christ.

Christian initiation, then, consists of the reception of the sacraments of baptism, confirmation, and the Holy Eucharist. These are the rites of initiation which, in the case of adults, were formerly preceded by a more or less lengthy preparation or catechumenate.

In the early Church there was no interval, as there is now in the Western Church, between these three sacraments; they were given in the same liturgical service. In this way, the unity of the rites of initiation, forming one process of initiation, was emphasised much more than the distinction between the sacraments.

Tertullian, writing at the end of the second century, expressed this in one sentence:

> The body is washed so that the soul may be purified; the body is anointed so that the soul may be made holy; the sign of the cross is made on the body so that the soul may be strengthened; the imposition of hands overshadows the body so that the soul may be enlightened by the Holy Spirit; the body is nourished by the body and blood of Christ so that the soul may feed on God.[2]

Christian initiation is initiation into the mystery which is the Church as well as introduction to the rich mysteries of sacramental life, especially the Holy Eucharist, the key mystery of the Catholic religion, so sacred that in the early Church its very existence was hidden under the "disciplina arcani," "the discipline of the secret," only to be revealed to those fully initiated by baptism and confirmation.

The revived interest in the rites of initiation and a desire for their renewal have come as a result of the liturgical revival of the past sixty years.

Even before the Vatican Council, the impact of this renewal had been felt and various measures had been taken to make the liturgical life of the Church more meaningful and more in keeping with the teaching of the Church through the ages and with the vision of Christianity expressed by the Fathers.

[2] Tertullian, *De Resurrectione*, 8, *Patrologia Latina*, 2806.

The great liturgical encyclical *Mediator Dei*, issued on 20th November, 1947, was a great step towards this goal. The Vatican Council Constitution on the Liturgy (*Sacrosanctum Concilium*), however, is a still greater step forward: it is the blueprint for such restoration.

The Council has outlined the plan for a complete renewal of Catholic worship and in so doing has put the stamp of the supreme authority in the Church—the Pope, together with the Bishops in council—upon the main insights of the liturgical movement. The document on the Liturgy must, of course, be read in conjunction with the other documents of the Council, especially the magistral *Lumen Gentium*, the Dogmatic Constitution on the Church. However, the principles put forward by the Council's document on the liturgy go far beyond practical reforms, or the remodelling of the liturgy: they reach down to the very bases of the whole of Christian spirituality and doctrine.

As Fr Bouyer says,

> Pope Pius XII had already done something along those lines in his famous encyclical *Mediator Dei*. But the doctrine of the Conciliar Constitution is much more elaborated and is made explicit in a text which is not only a fatherly exhortation—however enhanced it may have been by the papal authority responsible for it—but a most solemn expression of the whole teaching Church.[3]

This Constitution is a statement of the Church's belief about what she means and intends by her liturgy. It is the fundamental teaching concerning what she *does* in her worship. According to the principle that the nature of a thing can be deduced from how it works ("operare sequitur esse"), the Liturgy Constitution throws light on the very nature of the Church—and the Dogmatic Constitution on the Church throws great light on the Liturgy Conciliar document.

In this book, the Council documents on the Liturgy and the Church, and also on the Missions and on the Church in the Modern World, will be referred to in the appropriate places for their teaching on specific aspects of Christian

[3] Louis Bouyer, *The Liturgy Revived* (Notre Dame, Ind.: Notre Dame University Press, 1964), pp. 5–6.

initiation. However, it is important to stress that one must always keep in mind the fundamental principles of the Liturgy Constitution and of other Council documents. The initiate must be familiar with the Church's solemn, most recent statements of her teaching in order to understand the nature of the Church he is entering, its missionary character, and its role in the world today.

With regard to liturgy, these documents, and the Liturgy Constitution in particular, make it very clear that the liturgical renewal is neither the preserve of a handful of scholars, nor an attempt to revive something out of the past.

The teaching of the Council as expressed in the Liturgy Constitution may be summarised in five points.

1. The liturgy is the embodiment of the great mystery of our faith, the source of all our spiritual life as Christians, what the Council calls the Paschal mystery of Christ, his dying and rising again for our salvation. St Paul, in speaking of the Resurrection, says that if Christ is not risen then our faith is vain. He is not thinking of the Resurrection primarily as an apologetic proof of the divinity of Christ. He means that if Christ had not risen from the dead, there could be no such thing as Christianity because the central mystery of our salvation would have no existence. No one can be a Catholic who denies the Resurrection, this central mystery of our faith and of the whole liturgy—and the rites of Christian initiation make this clear.

2. This mystery is properly the mystery of worship, not only because it is fundamental to the worship of the Church but because it makes of all the members of the Church those worshipers in spirit and truth that the Father is seeking.

3. The liturgical mystery is also the mystery of the Church, not only because its proclamation to the world and its perpetual celebration are the great ministry committed to her care, her apostolic function, but also because it is the mystery of her own life, of her fusion into the mystical body of Christ itself.

4. The liturgy plays a central role in the whole activity of the Church. The Council explains it as a summit to which all the missionary activities of the Church are to lead and,

at the same time, as a source from which the whole Christian
life is to flow.

5. Finally, the Council makes plain that the liturgy, besides
presenting the mystery to us objectively in its sacramental
embodiment, is intended to enhance our personal reception
of it: our subjective response to God's great gift of grace.[4]

This view of the liturgy, as I have already stressed, can
no longer be regarded as if it were the view of pioneers, or as
something cranky, abstract, fanciful or obsolete. It is *the*
view of the whole Church and will never be changed, though
it may be developed and its implications more fully realised
in the future. We now see that attitudes towards the liturgy
in recent centuries have been imperfect. Theology has been
divorced from the living liturgy and has obscured the full
meaning of Christian truth; it has not been sufficiently
Biblical.

It is the sterile, abstract presentation of modern manuals
which is now regarded as insufficient and obsolete or, in
the words of Bouyer, as "a dry collection of correct but
uninspiring formulae which stink up the atmosphere of the
classroom and retain very little of the fragrance of God's own
words." [5]

The five general principles listed above should be kept in
mind as we approach the sacraments of Christian initiation.

[4] Cf. Bouyer, *op. cit.*, pp. 7–8, to which I am indebted for this
summary.

[5] *Ibid.*, p. 26.

PART ONE

THE SACRAMENTS OF INITIATION

CHAPTER I

A RICH HERITAGE

Baptism is the sacrament of the beginning of new life, the life of faith, the entrance into the kingdom of God. ". . . Unless a man is born through water and the Spirit he cannot enter the kingdom of God" (John 3:5).

Baptism is therefore the first sacrament in time and, in one way, in importance, for it is the rite of initiation *par excellence* into the earthly kingdom of God, the Church, and the precondition for receiving the spiritual riches of that kingdom, the kingdom of light, the start of a new existence. By baptism, a person begins to live as a child of God, as a member of a new supernatural world, initiated into the Paschal mystery of Christ and his mystical body.

In modern times the practice of infant baptism has tended to obscure the riches of this sacrament, its community nature has been weakened and the symbolism of its ceremonies lost, to a certain extent, because it has become a private ceremony in a strange tongue, often hurried through in a perfunctory manner. In order to recapture the depth and significance of the sacrament and its ceremonies and to restore it to its fundamentally important position, it is necessary to study the meaning of baptism in the New Testament, in apostolic times and in the first centuries of the Church's existence. Also we need to acquire an understanding of the Biblical riches which the symbolism of baptism draws on and which give significance to rites that otherwise do not have much meaning for modern participants. The meaning of baptism has not been completely lost; its vital role has always been acknowledged, but its meaning as a rite of initiation into the community of the people of God has not been stressed sufficiently, to the great loss of the Christian Church. The loss is especially serious for laymen in the Church, whose dignity is founded on their baptism, as St Peter testifies: "You are a chosen race, a holy people, a royal priesthood, a consecrated nation, a people set apart to sing the praises of God, who has called you *out of darkness into his wonderful light*" (I Peter 2:9).

All this understanding may be necessary, but is it possible? Our civilisation is different from that of Biblical times; a person may object that such a study and such an understanding are only for the liturgical historian or the ecclesiological antiquarian and that even for them such work may represent a retreat from the present into a past which is out of tune with the modern day. Biblical imagery can, at times, be so anachronistic as to verge on the ridiculous, when it is the sublime that should be perceived. To ask any but a highly educated audience in an urban milieu to say or sing "As the doe longs for running streams, so longs my soul for you, my God" risks not only unintelligibility but the reflection that religion which uses such language is irrelevant in a technological age. In a modern city, with water on tap, "a cup of cold water" can hardly have the evocative meaning that it had in a land and at a time when real thirst was no uncommon experience.

However, we must not exaggerate this difficulty. The images used in the sacraments of initiation are *not* recondite or bizarre but are easily intelligible, basic, primitive images which appeal to every culture.[1]

A more important reason why Biblical imagery should not repel the modern reader is that the Bible itself is the book of the People of God: to ponder on its themes and its imagery is not to go in for an optional study of historical writings. Knowledge of it is an essential part of the mental, spiritual and cultural equipment of a Christian. For the Bible is more than a narrative of historical events long past. It is the history of God's dealings with mankind, of the revelation that reaches from the creation to the Incarnation and beyond.

[1] Cf. Charles Davis, *The Making of a Christian* (London and New York: Sheed & Ward, 1964), pp. 6–7.

This is what we call salvation history, a special and unique kind of history in which events recorded had not only their usual historical sequence but were part of a plan of revelation, of God's approach to man, of his will to bring salvation to all mankind. This revelation was given not only in words but in historical events which were also symbols of a greater event to come.

For example, the Exodus (the miraculous intervention by God to rescue the Jews from their bondage in Egypt and bring them to the promised land through the passage of the Red Sea and the journey across the desert of Sinai) was an historic event of key importance in the history of the Jews. But it was also a type of the passage which Christ made by passing through the waters of death to his glorious reign after the Resurrection. It was also a type of baptism, by which the baptised "pass over" to the kingdom of God through the power of Christ's own death and resurection. The Exodus, far from being a dead event of past history, was remembered and "relived" by the Jews and taken over by the Christian Church so that it forms one of the most important elements of the solemn Easter vigil of our own days.

The Bible, in its grand themes—Old Testament and New —is the record of *our* history, it is our spiritual heritage.

> Where a community expresses its belief and worship in developed symbols as Christians do in the sacraments, this presupposes a common mentality. And a common mentality demands a common fund of words, a common memory of past great events and a common store of images and themes. Without such a common mentality symbolic communication, other than the crudest, is simply not feasible. Have Christians as a body such a common mentality? In theory, yes. The mentality that is supposedly ours, that must be ours if we are to take part intelligently in the sacraments, is that found in the Bible. The Bible—read by the Church, of course—gives us our common spiritual culture.[2]

But, of course, this does not mean the Bible is to be read in a fundamentalist way, as if every word were inspired, every sentence relevant to our own day, every book of equal

[2] Davis, *op. cit.*, p. 4.

value for ourselves. The pious custom which once obtained of reading the Bible from end to end, starting at Genesis and finishing at the Apocalypse, was perhaps a good exercise to gain familiarity with the Word of God, but it resembles the attitude of one who would seek general knowledge by reading an encyclopedia from A to Z. It should be admitted that there is much in the Old Testament that has no relevance, that has become a dead letter, that is even harmful in Christian times if read without discretion. Very queer aberrations have followed the adopting of some Old Testament ideas in modern times: they have even been used to justify oppression, tyranny, and racism (*Apartheid* in its origins in South Africa owes much to mistaken Biblical interpretation).

Our Lord warned us that the letter kills, it is the spirit which gives life. A trivial example of the neglect of this principle is the importance given in modern times to the rule that women should wear hats in church, in obedience to the letter of St Paul's injunction.

But the grand themes of the Bible—and many of the lesser illustration of them—have a perennial freshness and relevance. In the example "As the doe longs for running streams . . . ," it does not need much imagination—even though the image may be a strange one to many modern urban men—to realise that the Psalmist's main point is not the image he uses of the doe, but the intense longing for God which is common to him and his day, and to us and our day.

Hence our conditions of life, though so different from those of the Hebrews, with some instruction, study and effort need not be, *must* not be, an obstacle to our entering into the heritage of our Christian Biblical culture. It is true that some of the symbols in the sacraments, for example, may not come naturally to us, as they would have done to a Jew of the first century; knowledge and appreciation of them must be acquired. Some may even be discarded without great loss. But in most cases, understanding of such symbols is a worthwhile, indeed a necessary, thing for the modern Christian.

We must remember that God has made the Bible the permanent vehicle of his revelation, the permanent expression of his message. It is for all ages the Word of God. We must indeed transpose its teaching into other terms to meet fresh problems, to draw out its meaning, to relate it to advances in human thought and to present it in a language they understand to men who would otherwise find it unintelligible. But for Christians within the Church the Bible as it stands, with its own themes and images, remains the privileged expression of her faith, the raw material as it were of the Church's prayer, the source of her sacramental symbolism.[3]

The further time carries us from the Biblical era, the more difficult this task might seem to be. But providentially, in recent years, Biblical studies, modern translations, and a deeper understanding of the literary and historical context of the sacred books have given this generation, more than any previous generation of Christians, a full opportunity to understand the riches of the sacred books.

We can better appreciate the importance of a return to Biblical and early Christian sources with regard to the rites of Christian initiation through an analogy with the rites of initiation in tribal societies and pagan religions. These rites are steeped in folklore, the orally remembered history of the tribe linked to myths about the origin of the tribe and its customs. This folklore loses itself in the mists of time, yet it supplies the sanction, and at times the material, for the rites of initiation even at the present day.

To recapture the full meaning of the rites of Christian initiation we must go back to the New Testament—with its roots in the Old—and the writings and practice of the early Church, especially of the Fathers. This does not mean, as I have said, the professional historian's nostalgic return to the past. Nor does it involve an effort to restore ancient rites in their entirety, with an antiquarian's care, so that modern baptismal rites anachronistically become a replica of all that was practised in the early Church. The purpose of such a return must be a desire for a greater understanding of the meaning and origin of ceremonies we now have and, at the same time, a study of how the rites of our day can be revised and adapted to maintain the spirit of the early days and still fit meaningfully into the circumstances of life in the twentieth century and into the various cultures existing today.

[3] Davis, *op. cit.*, p. 6.

In doing this, we shall find that the symbols of the past will not be so difficult to comprehend, precisely because the main symbols of the sacraments of initiation are basic human symbols, common to men of all times.

For example, water, the main visible material element in baptism, has to all human beings a twofold symbolic meaning: of destruction and of life.

As I write, the world is shocked by the news of the terrible destruction of life and property caused by the worst Italian floods in history. The destructive properties of water are as clear to modern people as they were to the Psalmist. On the other hand, water in the form of irrigation is the key to life and abundance. I can think of a village in India which, in the famine of 1965, had plenty of food, because this village had been helped to establish water conservation and irrigation works while, a few miles away, Indians were dying of starvation because their crops had failed through lack of water.

CHAPTER II

BAPTISM IN THE BIBLE

We shall now consider (1) baptism in the Old Testament, and (2) baptism in the New Testament; under the latter heading we shall discuss (a) the baptism of John, (b) the baptism of Jesus, (c) Christian baptism in the New Testament, and (d) baptismal symbolism in St Paul's epistles.

BAPTISM IN THE OLD TESTAMENT

The sacramental rite of baptism was foreshadowed in the Old Testament: first of all obscurely in the ceremonial washing, which was intended to give ritual purity to persons or objects that had been defiled by contact with what was impure or unclean according to the Law. Ceremonial washing was necessary for priest and Levite before they could take part in the sacrifices. Another example that springs readily to mind is the purification after childbirth. However, the connection between ritual cleanliness and cleanliness of heart was not stressed at first. Indeed, the idea of these impurities was that they were attached to certain things or acts and a man could become "unclean" by simple contact with unclean things. Animals were divided into pure and impure. Contact with leprosy or with a corpse involved uncleanliness. A man who had contact with uncleanliness had to purify himself by a ritual washing, especially if he was going to approach God in a special way. Although these ideas may seem rather bizarre to us nowadays, they did instil the idea that God and his people are holy, and so his people must avoid contact with uncleanliness or purify themselves if they have become "unclean." This uncleanliness was clearly a ritual thing: it had nothing to do with moral fault, indeed it could be contracted accidentally and, as I have said, it was even applied to things. Incidentally, these ritual impurities were not always arbitrary—they were often sensible hygienic rules which, in a theocracy, naturally took on a religious significance.

The prophets, especially Isaiah and Ezekiel, began to make it clear that ritual purity was as nothing, even though so much weight was given to it, compared to spiritual purity. In Isaiah we read: "Your hands are covered with blood, wash, make yourselves clean. Take your wrong doing out of my sight. Cease to do evil. Learn to do good" (Isaiah 1:15–17). There are many texts in the Prophets of a similar nature.

The Prophet Ezekiel marks a landmark in this development. In his efforts to spiritualise ceremonial washing, he prophesied the institution of a new washing which would purify the soul as well as the body:

> I shall pour clean water over you and you will be cleansed; I shall cleanse you of all your defilement and all your idols. I shall give you a new heart and put a new spirit in you; I shall remove the heart of stone from your bodies and give you a heart of flesh instead (Ezekiel 36:25–26).

Here there is a foreshadowing of the outpouring of the Holy Spirit that is essentially connected with Christian baptism in the New Testament.

Nevertheless, in official Judaism, religious baths were intended to bring about a state of spiritual nearness to God, or rather, were necessary in order to allow one to attempt that nearness, and that religious nearness was not identified with moral purity. The rites which assured ritual purity might be signs of inward purity, but they did not bring it about.

At the time of Our Lord, the Pharisees had revived and greatly extended the need for and the scope of these rites. It was for this reason that Our Lord found it necessary to stress that external ceremonies did not cleanse a man's soul, just as lack of the external ceremonial of washing did not cause a man to be really defiled.

There was another kind of washing or baptism in the Old Testament, by means of which converts to Judaism were initiated into membership in the chosen race. These converts

had to take a ceremonial bath, which was preceded by instruction in the faith of Israel and by a test of the candidate's
sincerity. The candidate was received by the administering of
the ceremonial rite after a reading from the Law.

These recruits to the Jewish religion—especially numerous
about the time of Our Lord—were called "proselytes of justice." They were completely integrated into the Jewish faith
and had the same rites and duties as true Israelites. They
were circumcised and baptised. Sometimes, according to J.
Delorme, their baptism seems to have been more important
than their circumcision.

There is, therefore, a continuing development from Old
Testament ceremonies to the baptism of St John, to the baptism of Christ, and to Christian baptism.

The Qumran documents and other texts give evidence of
communities existing from the second century B.C. to A.D.
70 that made much of ritual purification. Although their
baths of purification were not purely ritual and implied a
relationship with conversion and interior purification, this
form of "baptism," earlier than the baptism of John, was not
a true rite of initiation. By its more frequent—possibly daily
—practice, it remained a ritual of simple purification.[1]

BAPTISM IN THE NEW TESTAMENT

The Baptism of John

The baptism of John is described by the Evangelists as
a baptism of repentance and of Messianic preparation. There
are two features which distinguish John's baptism. First, the
fact that he baptised others. In the purifications which were
common among Jews of the time, they bathed themselves,
and this was the case even in the "baptism" of proselytes.
Second, as precursor of the Messiah, which he openly claimed
to be—at least to those who understood the scriptures—he

[1] Cf. J. Delorme, "Baptism in Judaism," in A. George, S.M., and
others, *Baptism in the New Testament* (London: Geoffrey Chapman,
1964), pp. 25 ff.

was known by the rite which he performed: John the Baptist. Second, he preached his baptism as God's final saving intervention among his chosen people, as the final purification offered to them by the herald who was announcing the coming of the Messianic kingdom: a fulfilment of the prophecies of Isaiah, Ezekiel and Zachariah that God would one day carry out an immense washing of his people.

John's baptism was a baptism of "repentance for the forgiveness of sins" and a return to God, the classic message of the Prophets. This message was more insistent because this was the last chance, for public sinners, for pagans, even for the descendants of Abraham who thought themselves just, to prepare themselves for one who was already in their midst, the one whom all the prophets had foretold and of whom John was the forerunner—the Messiah. That was the peculiar significance of John's baptism. It was performed in preparation for one . . . "who is more powerful than I am, and I am not fit to kneel down and undo the strap of his sandals" (Mark 1:7)—to make ready for the Lord a people prepared, by his provisional baptism, for the one to come after him who would baptise with the Messianic baptism in the Holy Spirit and in fire.

The particular form that baptism was to take could not be known to John. Delorme says, "Christian baptism is closely linked with John's baptism. But between the two there had come the Passion and Resurrection of Jesus. To the 'baptism of John' there has succeeded baptism 'in the name of Jesus.' " [2]

There are many similarities and many differences between John's baptism and Christian baptism. Both involve the baptism of water and were conferred in view of Messianic times, both were a "baptism of repentance" marking an end of an age of sin for the individual, as well as for the world, and the beginning of a new life and a new age. Both were once-for-all actions, initiation rites of a new community of believers.

The differences, however, far exceed the resemblances. A

[2] Delorme, *op. cit.*, p. 60.

closer examination shows that the baptism of John consistently falls short of the Christian baptism. It is the shadow, whereas "baptism in the name of Jesus" is the reality. The "friend of the Bridegroom" must not be confused with the Bridegroom himself. John's baptism was a call to repentance, but it could not effect repentance; it signified a change of heart but did not bring that change about—only Christ's baptism could do that, because Christ's baptism is in the Holy Spirit. The gift of the Spirit makes the difference. Christian baptism is the baptism into the glorified humanity of Christ. John himself put his finger on the difference when he said, "I baptise with water but He will baptise you with the Holy Spirit."

In Christian baptism washing with water in the name of Jesus is the outward sign of the true inward washing that is done by the power of the Spirit. Christian baptism does more than introduce one into a new way of life: it effects a radical transformation and is a new birth because it joins us to the death and Resurrection of Christ.[3]

The Baptism of Jesus

All the synoptic Gospels regard the fact that Jesus submitted to the baptism of John as a very important event. St John the Evangelist did not go into detail about the actual baptism, but he too stressed the events that accompanied it.

The baptism of Jesus was an event of the greatest significance for the ministry of Jesus. It was also the first step in the institution of Christian baptism. It was a foreshadowing of that baptism, but at the same time it was one of those actions of Christ that were not only symbolic but effective. The Fathers saw not only the symbolism but also the first stage in the institution of Christian baptism. Christ received it to manifest what was to come and to inaugurate the work of bringing the new reality.

In the account given in Mark 1:9–11, the descent of the Holy Spirit in the form of a dove is seen, a prelude to the

[3] Cf. William J. O'Shea, *Sacraments of Initiation* (Englewood Cliffs, N.J.: Prentice Hall, 1966), p. 17.

baptism of the Holy Spirit which the Messiah would inaugurate. The dove was a familiar symbol of the spirit in Jewish tradition.

The acknowledgement of Jesus as his son by the Father during this baptism marks the beginning of the Messianic mission of Jesus. The going down into the waters and the coming out of them symbolises the other "baptism" with which he has to be baptised—the death on the Cross—and foreshadows the connection between Christian baptism and the death and Resurrection of Christ.

The reason Christ submitted to the baptism, St Ambrose points out, is not that he needed baptism (for he was without sin) but that we do. The text of St Ambrose is significant because it places the institution of baptism at the time of baptism by John.

> . . . When Christ Our Lord instituted the rite of baptism, he came to John and John said to him, "I should be baptised by you and you come to me." Christ replied, "Let it be so; for so must all justice be fulfilled." You see that all justice is founded on baptism.
>
> Why then did Christ go down into the water if not that the flesh should be purified, that flesh which he took of our condition? Christ had no need to be purified from sin—he who committed no sin—but we have need of it because we remain subject to sin. Just as it was for us that he instituted the rite of baptism so it was to our faith that this fulfilment of the rite was proposed.[4]

By taking his place with sinners in submitting to John's baptism, Christ identified himself, according to the will of the Father, with those he was about to save by taking on himself, as the Lamb of God, the sins of the world. By allowing John to baptise him he achieved that solidarity with the community he had come to save.

All the elements of Christian baptism are there: the water and the Holy Spirit, Christ the Son, and the Father. This is the manifestation of the Trinity in the name of which baptism is given.

[4] St Ambrose, *De Sacramentis*, Bk. 1, Nos. 15, 16, in Dom Bernard Botte, *Ambroise de Milan, Des Sacraments, des Mystères* (Paris: Editions du Cerf, 1961), p. 68.

The baptism of Christ in the Jordan made use, in an outstanding way, of water as a symbol of destruction and as a means of giving life. Christ, descending into the waters of the Jordan, was symbolising the pain and anguish that would overwhelm him on the cross, and his burial in the water was a symbol of his burial in the tomb. As he came out of the water the Spirit rested upon him in the form of a dove. This part of the incident suggested his emergence from the tomb and his glorification at the right hand of God.

There is a rather puzzling passage in John 3:22–26, in which we are told that Jesus caused his disciples to baptise just as John did. The Evangelist goes on to make clear that Jesus himself did not baptise, but only his disciples (4:2). This baptism must have been analogous to that of John the Baptist, for John the Evangelist laid stress on the Paschal character of the gift of the Spirit (7:39; 16:7; 20:22) and therefore there was not, nor could there be, baptism in the Spirit before the Resurrection.

Christian Baptism in the New Testament

As we have seen, Christ allowed his apostles to baptise while he was still alive, but this too was only a foreshadowing of true Christian baptism of water and the Holy Spirit. Incidentally, in their writings, the apostles are careful to distinguish between the original and unique nature of Christian baptism and the baptism of John, in spite of the importance they give to the latter.

St Ambrose, as we have seen, gives the impression that Christian baptism, as known to him, was instituted at the time of Jesus' baptism by John the Baptist; but it is probably better to see the institution of baptism as a complex of sayings and events in Our Lord's life culminating, after his death, in the apostles' realisation of what they had to do to admit believers into the infant Church.

In this line of development are the words of Jesus to Nicodemus: "Unless a man is born through water and the Spirit he cannot enter the kingdom of God" (John 3:5).

This referred to the earthly kingdom of God, it is clear,

for St Matthew's Gospel ends with the command of Christ to the apostles.

Jesus came up and spoke to them. He said, "All authority in heaven and on earth has been given to me. Go, therefore make disciples of all the nations, baptise them in the name of the Father and of the Son and of the Holy Spirit, and teach them to observe all the commands I gave you. And know that I am with you always, yes, to the end of time" (Matthew 28:18–20).

This text does not refer to the baptismal formula as we have it now, as if the command of Christ was to use those very words, but rather to the distinctive character of the baptism. Baptism was to be conferred on those who believed in the teaching, of Christ, especially the main part of it referring to the blessed Trinity.

The Gospels do not give us any precise moment when, from a legalistic point of view, we can say baptism was definitively instituted by Christ.

However, immediately after the descent of the Holy Spirit at the first Pentecost, the Acts of the Apostles record that, after Peter with the eleven had addressed the crowds in Jerusalem, three thousand were baptised. This was in answer to his appeal in the long speech in which he announced that Jesus, whom they had put to death, had been made, by the Father, Lord and Christ:

Hearing this they were cut to the heart and said to Peter and the Apostles "What must we do brothers?" "You must repent" Peter answered "and everyone of you must be baptised in the name of Jesus Christ for the forgiveness of your sins and you will receive the gift of the Holy Spirit. . . ." They were convinced by his arguments and they accepted what he said and were baptised. That very day about three thousand were added to their number (Acts 2:37–38, 41).

Here can be seen the classical pattern of Christian baptism: the preaching or kerygma, the profession of faith and the bathing with water, in this case probably by effusion or pouring of water rather than by immersion, which would have caused practical difficulties on account of the numbers.

The fact that the Apostles after the Resurrection baptised

and related this baptism to the gift of the Holy Spirit shows that they knew it was the will of Jesus that this was the way to admit others to the community of the infant Church of Christ. What they did was a fulfilment of the prophecy of John the Baptist (see Acts 11:15–17, quoted below).[5]

The teaching of the New Testament with regard to baptism and its effects is very rich but it is not of a formal nature; nowhere do the sacred writers set out to give a full account of baptism. The teaching comes incidentally—for example, in an exhortation to Christians to live a good Christian life, and thus be worthy of their baptism. Moreover, there are many texts which are not explicit but which may well apply to baptism and probably do. This is especially true of the Johannine epistles, which are full of symbolism.

Nevertheless, if we search the scriptures and collect those passages which definitely refer to baptism, a great body of profound teaching on this sacrament of Christian initiation can be assembled.

The book of the Acts of the Apostles (with all the literary strata which modern criticism distinguishes in that work today) gives an account of many baptisms. In Acts 8:12–17, the baptisms by Stephen's companions in Samaria are mentioned, and the way the apostles came from Jerusalem and completed them:

> But when they believed Philip's preaching of the Good News about the kingdom of God, and the name of Jesus Christ, they were baptised, both men and women, and even Simon himself became a believer. After his baptism, Simon who went round constantly with Philip was astonished when he saw the wonders and great miracles that took place.
>
> When the Apostles in Jerusalem heard that Samaria had accepted the Word of God, they sent Peter and John to them, and they went down there and prayed for the Samaritans to receive the Holy Spirit, for as yet he had not come down on any of them: they had only been baptised in the name of the Lord Jesus.

[5] A. George, S.M., in *Baptism in the New Testament,* p. 14, refers to J. Dupont, *Les problèmes du Livre des Actes* (Louvain, 1950).

Then they laid hands on them, and they received the Holy Spirit (Acts 8:12–17).

The baptism of the Ethiopian eunuch related in Acts 8:26–40 shows how the preaching of Philip met such good dispositions in this "God-fearing" man that any lengthy preparation was dispensed with; indeed, lengthy preparation only became necessary when neophytes did not have any background on which to build their Christian faith.

In Acts 9:1–19, the conversion of Saul is related at length and concludes: "So he was baptised there and then."

St Peter's baptism of the whole household of Cornelius, the first pagan to be baptised, was preceded by a whole series of revelations, described at the beginning of Acts, Chapter 10, which explain and stress the importance of what is happening. The chapter ends with the following passage.

> Could anyone refuse the water of baptism to these people now they have received the Holy Spirit just as much as we have?
> He then gave orders for them to be baptised in the name of Jesus Christ . . . (Acts 10:47–48).

In answer to Jewish critics of what he had done, Peter described what had happened to the Apostles in Jerusalem:

> I had scarcely begun to speak when the Holy Spirit came down on them in the same way as it came down on us at the beginning and I remembered that the Lord had said. "John baptised with water but you will be baptised with the Holy Spirit" (Acts 11:15–16).

Because of its fundamental importance in showing that the Church was open also to the Gentiles, the baptism of Cornelius took place in a unique, extraordinary and miraculous way, as had that of the apostles; Cornelius and his household received the Holy Spirit and became members of the Church *before* their actual baptism by water. Nevertheless they did receive baptism by water.

Other narratives of baptisms are found during the journeys of St Paul—for example, the baptism of Lydia and her household.

> One of these women was called Lydia, a devout woman from the town of Thyatira who was in the purple-dye trade. She listened to us and the Lord opened her heart to accept what

Paul was saying. After she and her household had been baptised, she sent us an invitation . . . (Acts 16:14–15).

Another example is the baptism of the gaoler at Philippi
and all that were in his house.

> The gaoler called for lights, then rushed in, threw himself
> trembling at the feet of Paul and Silas and escorted them out,
> saying, "Sirs, what must I do to be saved?" They told him
> "Become a believer in the Lord Jesus, and you will be saved
> and your household too." Then they preached the Word of
> the Lord to him and to all his family. Late as it was he took
> them to wash their wounds and was baptised there and then
> with all his household (Acts 16:29–33).

Baptisms at Ephesus and Corinth also took place on these
journeys (Acts 18:1–11; 19:1–7).

In this way we see the apostles and their disciples ful-
filling the injunction of Our Lord to baptise those whom they
converted.

These simple narrations of actual baptisms are comple-
mented by the recorded reflections of what baptism means
to a Christian that are contained in the New Testament, especially in St Paul.

It would be true to say that baptism is one of the main
themes of the Pauline epistles. A great number of passages
refer directly to it. There are many others which have the
doctrine of baptism as a background and many passing
references to baptism and its effects.

The Epistle to the Galatians gives quite a developed doctrine of baptism. In this teaching St Paul cites baptism as
the basis for his doctrine of adoption, of being clothed in
Christ, of sharing in the inheritance, and of the equality of
all members of the human race before God. There is a beautiful passage in the Epistle to the Romans (Chapter 6)
which develops the teaching of Galatians. Starting with God's
justification of man, Paul develops the whole idea of what
the Christian life is. The incorporation in Christ and being
made like the Saviour stems from baptism. This teaching finds
its completion in the eighth chapter, which describes the sort
of life the Christian, after his baptism, and under the inspiration of the Spirit, is enabled to live. The epistles to the
Corinthians, Ephesians, and Colossians and also the Epistle

to Titus confirm the statement that baptism is one of the main themes of the Pauline epistles. We find it mentioned also in the Epistle to the Hebrews.

The teaching of the New Testament with regard to baptism may be summarised as follows:

Baptism is the work of God, not man. It is in Christ that God the Father reconciles us with himself (II Corinthians 5:18–19). It is God who sends the transforming Spirit (Galatians 4:6; I Corinthians 6:11). Salvation comes from God (Titus 3:5).

The effectiveness of baptism comes from the most central mystery of our faith, that of Christ's death and Resurrection. We are plunged into Christ and incorporated into him in his death and Resurrection: "You have been buried with him when you were baptised: and by baptism too, you were raised up with him through your belief in the power of God who raised him from the dead" (Colossians 2:12).

The change brought about by baptism is a complete one, a total landmark in a man's life. The theme of "before" and "after" is one which we meet with again and again. *Before* we were slaves to sin. *Now* we are saints. Baptism is the dividing line. We pass from the old man to the new and baptism is our means of passage. Baptism strips the old man and clothes him with Christ: "If anyone is in Christ he is a new creature" (II Corinthians 5:17).

We used to be God's enemies, but baptism makes us his sons: "And you are, all of you, sons of God through faith in Christ Jesus. All baptised in Christ, you have all clothed yourselves in Christ" (Galatians 3:26–27). Now we are God's sons, adopted by him and united with Christ. All barriers have been destroyed: all that is left now is the one people of God.[6]

Baptismal Symbolism According to St Paul

St Paul conveys must of his teaching through a rich Biblically saturated symbolism.

Father Mollat, S.J., gives a good summing up of St Paul's attitude towards baptism in the various epistles. He says:

[6] Cf. Augustin Grail, O.P., in *Baptism in the New Testament*, p. 9.

To describe the transformation which baptism effects in the Christian, St. Paul sometimes uses spatial imagery. For instance: The Father . . . has delivered us from the dominion of darkness and transferred us to the Kingdom of his beloved Son. But more often than not, the Apostle expresses this temporal reality through the image of the two ages. For him, the Christian is a man who has passed from one age to another— from the age of sin to that of grace, from the age of Adam to that of Christ, from the age of the old man who was crucified on Calvary to that of the new man who was born on Easter morning. And baptism forms the frontier between these two ages. Through baptism man leaves one epoch for another —he changes his time; he rejects the past which belonged to sin, and enters the present which belongs to justice and salvation. The different baptismal symbols that we find in the epistles are simply different ways of expressing out of the night of the "world" which is travelling this astounding leap to perdition into the light of day which never ends. If we are to understand these symbols we must see them in this temporal context of past and present (of Paul's "remember what you once were" and "see what you have now become") in which most of them are set.[7]

The first symbol is that of *washing* or *purification*.

We have tended to give too restricted a meaning to this symbol, as if it referred merely to washing, without realising that in the sign or symbol of water there is a depth of meaning and a wide variety of significant application.[8] The symbolism which St Paul develops naturally grows out of the washing which is the central material fact that his converts experienced, and the dimension he gives to this idea is a good corrective of the restricted symbolism which is often attached to the washing.

The first aspect of baptism is, of course, the obvious one: ". . . you have been washed clean" (I Corinthians 6:11). The water of baptism cleanses: it is a bath which purifies. This is a natural symbolism familiar to Judaism as it is to many other religions. In the case of baptism, however, this symbolism goes beyond the ordinary ritual use of a bath. Christian baptism, unlike other ritual religious rites of wash-

[7] D. Mollat in *Baptism in the New Testament*, p. 63.

[8] Cf. Charles Davis, *The Making of a Christian* (London and New York: Sheed & Ward, 1964), pp. 1–3.

ing, is given only once, it is a unique event in the life of the initiates, whereas washing in the ordinary sense is often repeated—as were the ritual washings of Judaism and those referred to in the Qumram documents.

Christian baptism is more than a rite. It is an act of God which brings about what is signified: it is a sacrament. It causes a once-for-all change in the depths of a man's being. It is a profound ontological change, a change in being. As such, it is not repeated. The New Testament relates how Paul's own baptism washed him of his sins (Acts 22:16).

Another essential characteristic is that the baptismal washing is done "in the name of the Lord Jesus Christ" and of the Spirit of God. As D. Mollat says,

> This theological and liturgical formula explains the effectiveness of baptism. The invocation of the Lord Jesus Christ sums up the whole mystery of the Saviour; the name of Jesus recalls the reality of the Incarnation and the abasement it entailed; the title of Lord recalls the vivifying and sanctifying power of the resurrection; and the title of Messiah recalls the fulfilment, in the dead and risen Jesus, of the divine plan of salvation. It is from its unity with the redeeming act accomplished by the dead and risen Jesus that the baptismal ablution draws its power. On the other hand, this power is conferred on baptism by the Divine Spirit; it is the Spirit who acts in it, who washes, sanctifies and justifies. And since this Spirit is the "Spirit of our God"—that is, of the Father—the neophyte has his deepest being consecrated and directed to God. If the baptismal ablution is unique, sovereignly effective and absolutely original, it owes this fact both to its link with the redeeming cross and to its trinitarian character. By baptism, the neophyte is washed clean of the sins of the world from which he sprang and transferred to a world of new relationships, which unite him with the very life of God.[9]

In I Corinthians 6:9–10, St Paul goes out of his way to list the depravities to which the vicious of the pagan world were subject, in order to stress the efficacy of the washing that the Christians of Corinth received:

> You know perfectly well that people who do wrong will not inherit the kingdom of God: people of immoral lives, idolaters,

[9] D. Mollat in *Baptism in the New Testament,* pp. 66–67.

adulterers, catamites, sodomites, thieves, usurers, drunkards, slanderers and swindlers will never inherit the kingdom of God (I Corinthians 6:9–10).

This makes the contrast all the stronger when Paul says, in the next verse, "These are the sort of people that some of you were once, but now you have been washed clean and sanctified and justified through the name of the Lord Jesus Christ and through the Spirit of Our God" (I Corinthians 6:11). The converts who had come out of this society which was so full of vice had been washed clean of these sins by baptism and made part of the Messianic community, and of the "saints"—in this way becoming "holy" and "just" beings, with a share in the holiness and justice of God and so fit to approach him.

This sublime teaching on baptism is incidental to the point that Paul is making against the Christians of Corinth: they accuse each other before pagan tribunals. How can they do such things, he asks, since they are baptised and know what baptism means?

Subsequent verses add the teaching that the Christian must safeguard and preserve the purity that he has had conferred on him by baptism; nor must he think that, because of his baptism, he can do what he wishes, especially with his body. St Paul makes it clear that the purity gained by baptism concerns the body also. In Paul's teaching it is the whole man, body and soul, who is "purified, justified and sanctified" at baptism, and who therefore must be treated with the respect due to his divine vocation.

In Hebrews 10:22, there is reference to the same theme: So as we go in, let us be sincere in heart and filled with faith, our minds sprinkled and free from any trace of bad conscience and our bodies washed with pure water.

This verse shows the superiority of Christian baptism over former ritual washings and the ritual washings in vogue at the time. Baptism cleans the conscience as well as the body. It is a divine, a "pure" water, poured out on the body in order to purify the heart.

It recalls the prophecy of Ezekiel, to which reference has

already been made: "I shall pour clean water over you and you will be cleansed; I shall cleanse you of all your defilement and all your idols. I shall give you a new heart, and put a new spirit in you" (Ezekiel 36:25–26).

Christian baptism is the sacrament promised by Ezekiel, the effusion of the Spirit which is the sign of Messianic times. It is the sacrament of regeneration, which creates a new heart in man with which he can go to God with perfect confidence, it consecrates this renewed man to God.

> But when the kindness and love of God Our Saviour for mankind were revealed, it was not because he was concerned with any righteous actions we might have done ourselves; it was for no reason except his own compassion that he saved us by means of the cleansing waters of rebirth and by renewing us with the Holy Spirit which he has so generously poured over us through Jesus Christ our Saviour (Titus 3:4–6).

Regeneration and renewal: these two images stress that, thanks to the Spirit who acts through the water, man is no longer a creature of flesh but himself becomes spirit, one "born of God"; yet it is a renewal, because the man who emerges from the baptismal waters is the very man who was plunged into them.

This brings out the positive side of the symbolism of water. As we have already mentioned, water can be a symbol of life as well as of death. Here it is the symbol and the means of regeneration and renewal. Water—especially to the Jews, a people formed in the desert and in a land where water was still scarce and manifestly the source of life—was a symbol of life. Throughout the scriptures it has that meaning and the gift of the Spirit was compared to life-giving rain. A passage in Isaiah illustrates this life-giving and renewing power of water. The prophet gives this promise from God to the people in exile: "For I will pour out water on the thirsty soil, streams on the dry ground. I will pour my spirit on your descendants, my blessing on your children" (Isaiah 44:3).

St John in his Gospel explains that the fountain of living

water which Christ promised (John 7:37) is the Spirit coming to us from the risen Christ.

In the Epistle to the Ephesians, the community aspect of baptismal purification is seen with all its force.

> Husbands should love their wives just as Christ loved the Church and sacrificed himself for her to make her holy. He made her clean by washing her in water with a form of words so that when he took her to himself she would be glorious with no speck or wrinkle or anything like that, but holy and faultless (Ephesians 5:25–27).

It is the Church itself which is purified by the baptismal water: it washes away sin (every spot and blemish); it sanctifies: it renews; the result is that the Church emerges without wrinkle, young and vigorous, her life renewed.

The role of Christ in this is emphasised. It is his sacrifice that is at the root of the Church's sanctification and renewal. It is his redemptive death that gives the water its power. It is his love that does everything, and baptism is the constantly renewed sign of his love.

In Romans 6:3–4, Colossians 2:12, and Ephesians 2:5, another symbol is drawn from the baptismal bath which has a similarity with the ideas of certain pagan initiation rites. Here the symbol of water as a destructive element is used. Water is regarded here as the element of death.

> It represents the forces of dissolution and disintegration. The enemy of this world of order and form, it is the hostile power that strives to reduce all once more to formless chaos. To go down into water is to enter darkness and death; it is to be submerged in sea where all is dissolved.[10]

The plunging into and emerging from the baptismal water typify the sharing in Christ's death and Resurrection. The plunging into the water seen as a destructive element—a sign of death—typifies the neophyte's association with the dead and buried Christ. His rising out of the water typifies his solidarity with the risen Christ leaving the tomb, victorious over death. With Christ, he dies to sin and rises with him to a new life, "life with God" (Romans 6:10).

[10] Davis, *op. cit.*, p. 7.

Another Pauline symbol arises out of the convert's *stripping off his clothing* to go into the bath. When he came out of it "he put on Christ" as a new garment, so to speak. ". . . And you are, all of you, sons of God through faith in Christ Jesus. All baptised in Christ you have all clothed yourselves in Christ . . ." (Galatians 3:26–27).

This being clothed in Christ as in a new garment is associated by St Paul with the reform which must accompany and result from baptism. The Christians are expected to ". . . give up all things we prefer to do under cover of the dark" (Romans 13:12). They must break with former wicked ways. "Let your armour be the Lord Jesus Christ . . ." (Romans 13:14). In Colossians (3:9) the idea is developed further. At baptism a new relationship is created. The neophyte becomes one with him by a communion of life, by being inserted into, forming part of, Christ and thus a true heir to the divine inheritance.

From this union with Christ comes the close union of the baptised with each other, with the result that the divisions which normally separate men—religious, social, national, sexual—disappear. From the baptismal waters arises a reconciled humanity. Humanity is unified not with the abstract unit of a single category, but in the concrete and spiritual union of a multitude which has become one single person "by the presence of one single person in them all." Christ unifies humanity by uniting human beings to his own person, by his presence in them.[11]

From this union with Christ, humanity leaves the status of minor and slave, becomes adult and acquires the dignity of sonship. ". . . You are not a slave anymore; and if God has made you son, then he has made you heir" (Galatians 4:7).

A further consequence is drawn by St Paul from the symbol of stripping off clothing. This symbolism of putting off the "old man," a man of sin, of "flesh" (in the special Jewish meaning), and of culpable passions, makes baptism then a sacramental sign of the end of the world of sin and the

[11] Mollat, *op. cit.*, p. 73.

coming of an age of innocence and justice both for the human race and for the individual. The grace of baptism is the starting point for a progress which can have no end; it is a grace that demands striving on the part of man if he is to develop all its possibilities.

Another symbol of baptism used by St Paul (I Corinthians 10:1) is the crossing of the Red Sea, an event from salvation history which is an image of the passage from bondage to the promised land. This image is used by St Paul to warn the Corinthians against regarding baptism as a magical rite giving them permanent protection against every danger and infallibly guaranteeing them salvation. Against this "we are saved" mentality, St Paul uses the historical event to show that, as with the Hebrews (with most of whom God was not well pleased and who were punished in the wilderness), for whom God worked the miracle, so it is possible for a Christian, after being loaded with the gifts of baptism, to fall and cease "to please God." The significance of this passage is beautifully explained by Father Mollat.

> It is possible to draw a very complete theology of baptism from this reference to the Exodus. Through baptism the messianic community, which is made up of the Christian spiritual people, is taken under the divine cloud and united with its head, Christ the Saviour, passes from death to life. In this way God brings his plan to its fulfilment. But God's faithfulness calls for faithfulness on the part of the Christian, just as it had called for faithfulness on the part of their "fathers." Having benefited from the sacraments and passed through the water to the other side of death they must not rest on their victory, for their bodies like those of their fathers could still be overthrown in the wilderness through which the Church nourished with supernatural food makes its way.[12]

St Paul also uses the image of the *seal* to illustrate the radical change in status which is brought about by baptism. Later on this word was to have a technical meaning and to be used as another name for baptism. But in St Paul, especially in Ephesians, it is used as a symbol of the effects of baptism.

The seal is the presence of the Holy Spirit in the Christian

[12] Mollat, *op. cit.,* pp. 76–77.

—an active presence which gives the Christian a mark of holiness, of consecration to God, of being set apart for God.

This sealing sets the Christian apart from the unjust world and makes him a son of God and heir to the promise. In Ephesians 1:13, Paul says openly that baptism admits the Christian to the people of God—a new people of God indeed, but one having continuity with and inheriting the promises made to the old people of God. It is worth quoting the whole preceding passage to put this verse into its context.

Blessed be God the Father of our Lord Jesus Christ, who has blessed us with all the spiritual blessings of heaven in Christ. Before the world was made, he chose us, chose us in Christ, to be holy and spotless, and to live through love in his presence, determining that we should become his adopted sons, through Jesus Christ for his own kind purposes, to make us praise the glory of his grace, his free gift to us in the Beloved, in whom, through his blood, we gain our freedom, the forgiveness of our sins.

Such is the richness of the grace which he has showered on us in all wisdom and insight. He has let us know the mystery of his purpose, the hidden plan he so kindly made in Christ from the beginning to act upon when the times had run their course to the end: that he would bring everything together under Christ, as head, everything in the heavens and everything on earth. And it is in him that we were claimed as God's own, chosen from the beginning, under the pre-determined plan of the one who guides all things as he decides by his own will; chosen to be for his greater glory, the people who would put their hopes in Christ before he came.

Now you too, in him, have heard the message of the truth and the good news of your salvation, and have believed it; and you too have been stamped with the seal of the Holy Spirit of the Promise, the pledge of our inheritance, which brings freedom for those whom God has taken for his own, to make his glory praised (Ephesians 1:3–14).

There seems little doubt that the seal here refers to baptism. After the preaching of the Gospel, which was received with faith by these pagans to whom Paul is writing, the Spirit sealed them as believers and they were thus admitted or initiated into the Church.

According to Father Mollat, the most characteristic ideas

of the theology of the covenant appear here one after the other: after references to the blessing and to election come references to the promise, the inheritance, redemption and the people which God had acquired for himself. All the religious privileges of old Israel are transferred to the Christians, the true beneficiaries of the blessings promised in Abraham to all the nations of the world. And it is the Holy Spirit who "signs" the baptised for this inheritance, and already communicates the first fruits of it to them by his own presence. Sealed with the seal of the promise and thus made the true spiritual posterity of Abraham, Christians are again marked by the Spirit for a full redemption on the day when God will finally carry out his promise and give the full possession of the inheritance to those who belong to him.[13] This eschatological interpretation of the baptismal seal in the light of the promise and of the Exodus, is confirmed later in the Epistle.

St Paul refers to the seal again in Ephesians 4:30: "Otherwise you will only be grieving the Holy Spirit of God who has marked you with his seal for you to be set free when the day comes."

There seems to be a reference here to Isaiah 63:9 ff., in which the prophet, after mentioning the goodness which God had shown to his people, recalls their lack of gratitude and the divine punishment which followed. ". . . In his love and pity he redeemed them himself, he lifted them up, carried them, throughout the days of old. But they rebelled, they grieved his Holy Spirit. Then he turned enemy, and himself waged war on them" (Isaiah 63:9–10).

In Ephesians 4:30, St Paul is warning the Christians not to let a like fate overtake them. Even though they have been sealed with the Spirit at baptism, this will not shield them from the anger of God at the (eschatological) "day of redemption" unless they are faithful and avoid "grieving" God by their sins. The image of the seal recurs in the second Epistle to the Corinthians. "Remember it is God himself who assures us all, and you, of our standing in Christ, and has

[13] Mollat, op. cit., p. 79.

anointed us, marking us with his seal and giving us the pledge, the Spirit, that we carry in our hearts" (II Corinthians 1:21–22).

In this first chapter of his second Epistle to the Christians at Corinth, St Paul is insisting on the firmness and stability of his teaching about Christ against those adversaries who had accused him of pusillanimity. On the contrary, he declares, God has established him firmly in Christ as he has all Christians by the seal he has put upon them and by the gift of the Holy Spirit he has given them in baptism. This serves as a guarantee of the perfect fulfilment of God's promises.

A final symbol of baptism in St Paul is that of *light*. This symbol is used very early in the Church. St Justin calls baptism an "illumination." Ephesians 5:8–14 is the first occurrence of this symbolism; Christians must behave as those who were once "darkness" but are now children of "light."

> You were darkness once, but now you are light in the Lord; be like children of the light, for the effects of the light are seen in complete goodness and right living and truth. Try to discover what the Lord wants of you, having nothing to do with the futile works of darkness but exposing them by contrast (Ephesians 5:8–11).

The references in Ephesians 5:8–14 need not necessarily be applied to baptism but this is quite an apt interpretation, and it is strengthened when read in conjunction with two passages, in the letter to the Hebrews (10:32). "Remember all the sufferings that you had to meet after you received the light in earlier days. . . . Be as confident now, then, since the reward is so great. You will need endurance to do God's will and gain what he has promised" (Hebrews 10:32, 35–36).

In the verse "Remember all the sufferings that you had to meet after you received the light in the earlier days," "received the light" seems certainly to refer to their Christian initiation, to their baptism. St Paul is telling the Hebrews to remember when their baptism had been a source of strength and light to them. They are to let this light still guide and help them right up to the time when they will see the fulfilment of its promise—"You will need endurance to do God's will and gain what he has promised."

In Hebrews 6:4 there is another reference to light:

> As for those people who once were brought into the light, and tasted the gift from heaven, and received a share of the Holy Spirit, and appreciated the good message of God and the powers of the world to come and yet in spite of this have fallen away—it is impossible for them to be renewed a second time. They cannot be repentant if they have wilfully crucified the Son of God and openly mocked him (Hebrews 6:4–7).

This is again most probably a reference to baptism. If so, the meaning would be that baptism—enlightenment—is the supreme gift of God "to renew man" and deliver him from death. If this is rejected, if this grace is denied by a final act of apostasy, if the Christian turns his back on the baptismal light and rejects his only Saviour, then this would, by definition, plunge him into a night without hope.

CHAPTER III

THE LITURGY OF BAPTISM

BAPTISMAL LITURGY IN THE APOSTOLIC ERA

It is not only from the teaching in the New Testament that we get an insight into the meaning of baptism. The liturgy of baptism itself gives a very great deal of instruction with regard to the nature of the sacrament. In apostolic times two actions were regarded as essential, the bathing with water and the profession of faith. To this should be added the idea of repentance.

The Acts of the Apostles lay stress on the bathing with water and *its penitential aspect* (2:38; 2:16), but as we have seen, St Paul develops its meaning more fully. This penitential rite unites us with Christ and makes us participate in the mystery of his death and Resurrection (Romans 6:2–11; Galatians 3:27; I Corinthians 12:13; Ephesians 5:26; Colossians 2:11–13).

In Mark 16:15–16 and Matthew 28:19–20, the profession of faith is closely bound up with the rite of washing with water. St Matthew writes that the washing is made in the name of the Father and of the Son and of the Holy Spirit. He is not citing a liturgical form in use at that time, he is showing the object of the faith which the person who is being baptised must profess. St Paul also witnesses to the close link between the profession of faith and bathing with water (Galatians 3:26–27), and the connection is even more pronounced in the descriptions of Christian baptism in the Acts of the Apostles. According to the Acts of the Apostles, too, the object of faith is essentially the person of Christ. That is the meaning of St Paul's frequent use of the expression "to be baptised in the name of Jesus Christ." Again, it is important to note that this is not a liturgical formula but an indication of the object of the faith: Jesus the Saviour. The object of faith was not only Jesus but his relationship with the Father and the Holy Spirit (Acts 2:33) and the knowledge that he has become, by his Resurrection, the Messiah and Saviour, the source of salvation for all.[1]

PREPARATION FOR BAPTISM
IN APOSTOLIC TIMES

In apostolic times baptism was already preceded by a preparation and certain conditions were required. This preparation had no need to be a lengthy one, as can be seen from the baptisms at Pentecost and the baptism of the Ethiopian eunuch by Philip. Nevertheless, three preparatory acts or dispositions were required: repentance for sin, including the practice of the commandments according to St Matthew (28:19–20); faith; and the profession of faith, which was preceded by the apostolic preaching or instruction.

BAPTISM IN THE EARLY CHURCH

From the nature of things, with Christianity spreading through Roman society—indeed throughout the Roman Empire, beginning in the second half of the first century—adult baptisms were the usual thing. What happened to the children of believers with regard to baptism is not clear, but infant baptism was an accepted thing by the fourth century.

Most conversions involved pagan adults. Once the principle had been established that the Gentiles were to be admitted—with the baptism of Cornelius and the first Council of Jerusalem, this question was settled—the problem of preparation for baptism became a serious one. In the case of Jew-

[1] R. Béraudy "L'initiation chrétienne," in A. G. Martimort, ed., L'eglise en prière (Tournai: Desclée, 1965), p. 531. I wish to express my indebtedness to this book as a source for some of the following pages.

ish converts soaked in Biblical lore, all that was needed was the profession of faith that Jesus is the Lord, the Messiah. This sufficed for baptism. Further implications of this could and would be worked out in the apostolic preaching and in the various epistles.

Even pagans like Cornelius probably did not create much difficulty, for in all probability they were the "God-fearing" men among the pagans of the Roman Empire who had renounced the worship of the pagan gods of Rome and other deities and had accepted the true God of the Jews, even though they had not become, as the "proselytes" had, accepted into the Jewish religion.

Towards the end of the first century, at Rome and elsewhere, converts came from a completely pagan society, possibly without any knowledge of the history of the people of God, without a knowledge of the commandments of God and without any preparation to live the life of a Christian. What, in the time of the apostles, had been an adequate preparation was now too sketchy for this new type of convert. A whole gamut of instruction and a formal preparation for baptism were needed.

The Church gradually developed a lengthy probation period for teaching, self-discipline, and sacramental rites, or "sacramentals."

At the time of St Justin the Martyr, the middle of the second century, this period of preparation was in an embryonic state. The main lines of the future prebaptismal discipline, however, can already be discerned. This preparation consisted principally of teaching and prayer and fasting. The teaching explained the faith which would have to be professed at baptism and the moral conduct which would be expected of the convert as a Christian. In the early Church it was made very clear that the object of faith was not the learning of a body of truths—not a philosophy or an academic subject—but a way of life based on faith in life-giving truths which taught about a Saviour, a real person, who was not only the cause of salvation but a model to be imitated. It is very striking that, although in the Church of the Fathers there were outstanding intellects who could meet the most cultured men of their time on their own intellectual ground, the preparation for baptism which they refer to was never a sterile intellectual, apologetic training, but a training for life as a Christian. Fasting, as part of the discipline of this life, was fixed for the neophyte for Wednesday and Friday of each week.

By the third century, there had been a further development of this period of preparation, according to the *Apostolic Tradition* of Hippolytus. It had already become an organic institution.

The Prebaptismal Discipline According to Hippolytus (Third Century)

The prebaptismal discipline comprised two stages: a lengthy preparation or *catechumenate* in the true sense of the word, to which the catechumens are bound, and secondly a *proximate preparation,* really the second stage of the catechumenate, designed for those who were shortly to be baptised. The catechumenate was of varying lengths according to the dispositions of the candidate, but it did not exceed three years. It included education composed of the following elements: a moral instruction given by a teacher or catechist "which had for its object the preparation of the candidates preparatory to their being included in the class of those to be baptised." This comprised the prayer of the catechumens which was separate from that of the faithful, the laying on of hands and prayer over catechumens by the teacher.

The *proximate preparation* included the examination of the life of the candidates with a testimony from those who had brought them for instruction, the teaching of the Gospel, and daily exorcisms by the imposition of hands. As baptism approached, a more solemn exorcism was carried out by the bishop. On the Thursday preceding the actual baptism the candidates took a bath. They fasted on the Friday and Saturday. On the Saturday there was a preliminary gathering presided over by the bishop. This included a new laying on of hands, the breathing on the face, as well as the signing of the ears, the forehead and the nose. There was a vigil all through Saturday night during which there were readings and instructions. At dawn the assembly went to the baptismal font and the candidates for baptism disrobed. Before being plunged into the bath, they renounced Satan and were anointed by a priest with the "oil of exorcism." In early times, baptism could be given on any Sunday but very soon it came to be almost exclusively reserved for the Easter vigil.

The Full Rite of Baptism at Rome in the Fourth and Fifth Centuries

By this time in Rome and Milan the most complete development of the baptismal rite had occurred. From the end of the fifth century onwards modifications occurred to take into account the fact that the greater number of baptisms were those of new-born babies. Although some changes (in Gaul, for example) did add to the value of the ceremonies even from an adult point of view, on the whole it can be said that baptism in the fourth and fifth centuries represented the peak of baptismal ritual development.

It is possible to have a fairly complete idea of the baptismal liturgy and prebaptismal discipline from fragmentary testimonies of the Fathers (though the evidence from St Ambrose of Milan is really more than fragmentary) of a letter of the deacon called John to a certain Senarius, and from the ritual which is preserved in the *Gelasian Sacramentary* (of the seventh century).

As in the third century, the period of preparation was divided into two parts: the *catechumenate* or remote preparation of about three years' duration and the *proximate* preparation, which lasted the whole of Lent for the "electi" or those who had been chosen for baptism at the next Easter vigil.

The *catechumenate* was the period in which the catechumens were instructed at length in the scriptures of the Old Testament and the thought of the Jewish people prior to the coming of Christ. This instruction was given by a chief catechist or "doctor" who had the title of "instructor of the hearers." He was delegated by the bishop. At the end of each instruction a prayer was said and the catechist, often a layman, would give a blessing. The catechumens were allowed to take part in the first part of the eucharistic worship—"the service of the word," the Mass of the Catechumens. Incidentally, this was not only the first part of the Eucharistic celebration, although that is the form in which we know it today. It could be held as a separate "Bible service" in its own right. The instruction was mainly of a moral nature leading the catechumen to the living of a worthy Christian life.

The specific Christian doctrinal instruction was given mainly during the final stages of preparation. During the catechumenate the emphasis was on spiritual formation. Tertullian calls the catechumenate the novitiate of the Christian life. The readings were mainly from the books of the Old Testament which were useful for conveying moral instruction, e.g., the Wisdom books, Tobit, Judith, Esther.

But a catechumen had to meet a certain standard of conduct before he was admitted even to the catechumenate. He was vouched for when he wished to enter the catechumenate by a member of the Church or "guarantor" before the Christian assembly, especially the leader. He had to show that he was not working at any trade or profession unsuited to a Christian. In its origin this custom was probably not only a test of the moral conduct of the candidate, but a very necessary precautionary measure, at least until 325, when Constantine declared Christianity to be the religion of the Roman Empire. Up to that time, there had been ten main persecutions of the Christians in the Roman Empire. An unworthy or false catechumen, although kept by the "discipline of the secret" from knowing the most sacred Christian mysteries, could have done considerable damage to the Christian community in time of persecution or religious unrest merely by betraying the meeting place of the Christians.

This custom shows the community nature of the baptismal preparation. From the very first the candidate had the feeling of being initiated into a community, the members of which were concerned about him and anxious to help in his preparation. This became more obvious during the *proximate* preparation. Still, even on being admitted to the catechumenate, the neophyte was allowed to call himself a Christian, but he was not regarded as one of the *fideles* or faithful.

As we shall see, the baptismal ceremony was so impressive a break with the past, it emphasised so strongly that those baptised passed from their old life to a new life, and it was held in such great reverence that later on a number of catechumens did not pass beyond the stage of being catechumens when they had finished their course, preferring to remain in that state until near death or until the obstacles to leading a really "new" life had been removed.

By the fourth century, certain other sacramentals had been added to the ceremony of entry into the catechumenate already referred to by St Augustine.

According to the letter of John the Deacon, they were: a short catechesis about the rudiments of the faith and the commandments; then a breathing on the candidate (exsufflation) "to blow away Satan" with the exorcism *Omnipotens*; the imposing of the sign of the cross with the prayer *Preces Nostras*; and the ceremony of the blessing and the giving of salt. The ceremony ended with a closing blessing, *Deus Patrum Nostrum,* which still ends the first part of baptism today.[2]

The *proximate* preparation came after the examination of the conduct and dispositions of the candidate during his three-year catechumenate (which could be shortened for good reasons). The community character of this preparation is so pronounced that the liturgy of the Lenten Masses is partly unintelligible unless it is realised that the whole assembly or Church was joining in the preparation for the baptism of the chosen ones on the night of Holy Saturday. From the second century onwards, baptisms were carried out in common on the night of the Easter vigil; later the vigil of the Ephiphany and of Pentecost were sometimes also used.

The first ceremony in the proximate preparation or the preparation of the "chosen ones" was the inscribing of the

[2] All these prayers are still in use. See *Small Ritual* (London: Burns & Oates, 1964), pp. 8–12.

catechumen's name on the list of those to be baptised with the prayer *Deus qui humani generis.*

From the end of the fourth century the proximate preparation was confined to Lent. The Lenten liturgy is still full of the great baptismal themes. The preparation consisted of a moral and spiritual formation, a doctrinal formation, and a preparation by means of sacramentals. This information we have from St Leo, who says that the chosen ones must be "subjected to scrutinies with exorcisms, made holy by fasting and instructed by frequent preaching."

These "scrutinies" were not examinations of the candidates. Rather they were prayers of a special kind—exorcisms —intended to help the candidates in the struggle to lead a better life and overcome the evils of the devil. They were accompanied by the laying on of hands by the bishop or his representative, and the candidates were also signed with the sign of the cross.

The signing with the sign of the cross had a rich symbolism. In Gaul in the sixth century it included the following beautiful prayer, which came later into the Roman ritual:

> Receive the seal of Christ, listen to the divine words, be enlightened by the Word of the Lord, because today you are accepted by Christ.
>
> I sign your forehead in the name of the Father, the Son and the Holy Spirit so that you may be a Christian.
>
> I sign your eyes so that you may see the glory of God.
>
> I sign your ears, so that you may hear the voice of the Lord.
>
> I sign your nostrils so that you may breathe the fragrance of Christ.
>
> I sign your lips, so that you may speak the words of life.
>
> I sign your heart so that you may believe in the Holy Trinity.
>
> I sign your shoulders so that you bear the yoke of Christ's service.
>
> I sign your whole body, in the name of the Father, the Son and the Holy Spirit so that you may live for ever and ever.[3]

Different formularies were used for men and for women. According to the *Gelasian Sacramentary,* there were three

---

[3] Quoted by P. Paris in *L'initiation chrétienne* (Paris: Beauchesne et Fils, 1948), p. 26.

"scrutinies," on the third, fourth, and fifth Sundays of Lent, and each of these days had a special text of the Mass applying to this ceremony.[4] The ceremony closed with the prayer *Aeternam et Justissimam.*

These scrutinies were the spiritual complement of the personal efforts that the candidate was supposed to make during this solemn Lenten preparation for his baptism. During this time he gave himself up to greater spiritual efforts, fasted more frequently, observed the practice of the commandments with greater diligence. At the same time the whole Church was also intensifying its own spiritual efforts for Lent and in union with the ones chosen for baptism. During this time, as St Leo says, many doctrinal instructions were given. This was naturally the case because it was the main opportunity for the catechumens to receive instruction in the Christian faith. These instructions led up to the ceremony of the fifth Sunday of Lent (at Rome; in Africa the time was slightly different), when the "chosen" were given at least the Creed and possibly all three precious embodiments of the teaching of the Christian Church: the Creed, the Lord's Prayer, and the Gospels (the technical names were: *traditio symboli, traditio orationis dominicae* and *traditio Evangelii*). The Creed (the Apostles Creed) was recited in the presence of the "chosen" and explained by the celebrant (the same thing happened with regard to the Our Father), the Gospels were solemnly presented, extracts were read and homilies given. The "elect" had to learn the Creed and Our Father by heart, the former as a password (in Latin, "symbolum"—"password"), and be ready for the *Redditio,* i.e., the giving back, which took place at another ceremony, when they would recite the Creed and the Our Father before the Assembly. Probably all this took place on Passion Sunday.

On Holy Saturday morning a solemn final assembly took place. Between Passion Sunday and this meeting the "elect" had received detailed instructions on the Creed.

On Saturday morning they "gave back" what they had been taught, in the *Redditio Symboli.* This was the very

---

[4] For a full account of the "scrutinies" and the Masses connected with them, see R. Béraudy, *op. cit.,* pp. 538, 723–725.

solemn moment when the candidate affirmed his faith in what
he had learnt of the teaching of the Church and of the teaching of the Gospel, summarised in the Creed. This step
finally bound them to the Church and compromised them in
the eyes of the world (no mean step in the times of persecution). It also balanced the community nature of the baptismal ceremonies: this was an intensely individual act,
though carried out in the presence of the faithful. The cor-
porate nature of the saved people of God has never taken
on the characteristics of a mass movement or the emotional-
ism of the crowd. Here, at this most solemn moment, the
lonely, responsible individual choice is made, helped and encouraged by the worshipping community. But the individual
is not one of a crowd passively accepting a tradition, he is
freely accepting responsibility for his choice and at the same
time binding himself to a personal fulfilment of all that his
choice implies in the way of active belief and Christian conduct. The community nature of the Church is not meant to
dispense the Christian from personal effort, but to lead him
up to it, encourage, strengthen, and guide it and invoke the
blessing of God upon it.

Actually the ceremony of the *Redditio Symboli* came at
the end of the rite. First of all there was a final and more
solemn exorcism, a last effort of the Church to remove all
hindrance to a fruitful reception of baptism, which was to
take place that very night. Then the catechumens were
anointed with the oil of catechumens on ears, nose, and breasts
with the prayer *Ephpheta,* which is still used in our ritual.

The annointing was intended to symbolise the fact that,
although the catechumens were being exorcised, their struggle
with the powers of evil would last their whole lives. The oil
was like the oil of combat used by athletes before a contest.
In ancient times the body was anointed all over, not only on
the breast and between the shoulder blades. St Ambrose asks
in one of his catechetical sermons, *On the Sacraments,* "Why
are the nostrils anointed?" and he answers, "In order that
you might receive the blessed odour of the eternal goodness
and so that you may say 'We are the pleasing odour of

Christ for God', as the Holy Apostle says[5] and that there should be in you the full fragrance of faith and devotion."

Then came the solemn renouncing of Satan, all his works and all his pomps, in a three-fold renunciation. In this impressive rite the candidate first turned his face to the West, from which darkness comes with the setting of the sun and which therefore symbolised the realm of darkness, the realm of Satan. Then he was asked by name if he renounced Satan, which he solemnly did, rejecting Satan himself, his works or deeds, and his pomps. The meaning of the word "pomps" has become obscured. Originally it referred to the worship of the devil [6] but this came to mean the games in theatres and all the idolatrous worship linked to them.

This was the candidate's response, as it were, to all the exorcisms to which he had been exposed during his whole preparation and especially during Lent and in this ceremony. The Church had been praying that he might be preserved from the power of the devil, that evil might have no power of him. Here the candidate, strengthened by the prayers of the Church, freely declares himself to be on the side of God, vows to fight against the devil in active combat by his own free choice, to "put off the old man" and all evil conduct and "put on Christ": a choice which will be ratified by his personal encounter in the sacrament of baptism, by which Christ will make him partaker of his victory over evil. By Christ's victory the catechumen will be enabled to "put off the old man," as he has vowed.

As Louis Bouyer puts it, "No doubt the Church will continue to fight with him and for him. But he is now going to belong to the Church because in this struggle (against the devil and evil) he is no longer a passive stake but a clear-headed and conscious fighter".[7]

---

[5] In II Corinthians 2:15.

[6] See a fascinating chapter, "I renounce Satan, his Pomps, and his works," by M. E. Boissard in A. George, S.M., and others, *Baptism in the New Testament* (London: Geoffrey Chapman, 1964), pp. 107 ff.

[7] Louis Bouyer, *Christian Initiation* (London: Burns & Oates, 1960), p. 75.

THE PASCHAL VIGIL

The personification of the Paschal event is referred to in
I Corinthians 5:7. "Christ our passover has been sacrificed;
let us celebrate the feast then by getting rid of the old yeast
of evil, having only the unleavened bread of sincerity and
truth."

This celebration of the central mystery of the Christian
faith was the most solemn event of the year: as we shall see,
it was the setting for the solemn rites of Christian initiation.

The Vatican Council has restored to the Church the
realisation of the Paschal mystery in all its fundamental importance. This is especially clear in the Liturgy Constitution.

> Just as Christ was sent by the Father so also He sent the apos-
> tles filled with the Holy Spirit. This he did so that by preaching
> the Gospel to every creature (Mk. 16:15), they might pro-
> claim that the Son of God by his death and resurrection, had
> freed us from the power of Satan (Acts 26:18) and from
> death and had brought us into the kingdom of the Father. His
> purpose was also that they might exercise the work of salva-
> tion which they were proclaiming, by means of sacrifice and
> sacraments, around which the entire liturgical life revolves. . . .
>
> In like manner, as often as they eat the supper of the Lord,
> they proclaim the death of the Lord until he comes (I Cor.
> 11:26). For that reason on the very day of Pentecost, when
> the Church appeared before the world, "those who received
> the word 'of Peter' were baptised." And "they continued stead-
> fastly in the teaching of the apostles and in the communion
> of the breaking of the bread and in the prayers . . . praising
> God and being in favour with all the people" (Acts 2:41–47)
> (No. 6).

The rest of the paragraph goes on to explain what was
said in the first sentence of this chapter.

> From that time onward the Church has never failed to come
> together to celebrate the Paschal mystery: "reading" in all
> the scriptures the things referring to himself (Lk. 24:27),
> celebrating the eucharist in which "the victory and the tri-
> umph of his death are made present" (Council of Trent) and
> at the same time giving thanks "to God for his unspeakable

gift" (II Cor. 9:15) in Christ Jesus "to the praise of his glory" (Eph. 1:12) through the power of the Holy Spirit.[8]

We may pause here and consider the Paschal mystery which is commemorated by the Easter vigil and into which the "elect" were initiated.

First of all, the word "mystery" in this case does not mean anything mysterious, something which we cannot explain or even any truth which we must receive by faith because it is beyond our understanding. Still less does it mean the inner secrets of a religious cult that are to be reserved, away from the profane multitude, for a privileged and esoteric band of true initiates, as in some pagan religions.

The Christian religion has no "mystery" which is not open to the humblest believer as well as to the most exalted members of the hierarchy. The Pope is no more a baptised Christian than the simplest peasant's child, just baptised.

The Paschal mystery is the great secret of God's design for the salvation of the world. That secret, as Father Bouyer says, could not be discovered by the highest human wisdom. Indeed, it so far surpasses its capacity that once revealed, human wisdom cannot grasp it: the wise of this world are simply bewildered by its revelation. It seems like foolishness to them. And this is not surprising, for neither men—even the wisest among them—nor the angels themselves could achieve that knowledge without a special revelation of God, and the communication of his own Spirit.[9]

The Paschal mystery, in its realisation by Christ, was the culmination of God's plan of salvation, shown through the whole of scriptures, acted out in figure by the history of the Jews, the chosen people, for whom the Pasch or Passover was the most solemn event in their history, the most solemn commemorative feast of their religious year.

Originally the Pasch was simply a spring festival common in pagan religions. It was the festival of creation, life reap-

[8] Walter M. Abbot, S.J., ed., *The Documents of Vatican II* (New York, America Press, 1966), p. 140.

[9] L. Bouyer, *The Liturgy Revived* (Notre Dame, Ind.: Notre Dame University Press, 1964), p. 17.

pearing on the earth after the apparent death in winter. But after the captivity of the Israelites in Egypt and their miraculous deliverance (1230 B.C.),[10] the feast took on a new meaning. It commemorated what happened on the night when the Paschal meal was eaten by the Hebrews, and God "passed over" the houses of the Hebrews and slew the inhabitants of Egypt, thus preparing the way for the escape, or Exodus, of the Israelites from Egypt.

Furthermore, as Father Bouyer says, even in the Old Testament we find the idea that God, passing through Egypt and "passing over" the Israelites, caused them, together with himself, to pass from Egypt to the Red Sea and so to the land promised them at the other side of the desert of Sinai and of the River Jordan—and thus from the land of bondage to the land of freedom.

> And this, in itself, was much more than a merely material deliverance. It was a complete renewal (if not the total creation) of the filial consciousness of Israel towards its God. It was therefore a passage from darkness to light, from death to life. It was redemption in the basic meaning of the word: the ransom paid for the slave.[11]

The death of Christ on the cross on the eve of the Pasch is truly the Paschal mystery, not just because it happened on the day that the Paschal lamb was immolated, but because in the Old Testament the celebration of the Pasch had from the beginning pointed to the cross. The mystery of the cross underlies this historic event which prepared for it, promised it, anticipated it, for the faithful people of God.

As we have seen and will see again, the rites of initiation make much of this central Paschal mystery. The Easter vigil was not merely a commemoration of what was past. As the Liturgy Constitution says, in the Christian celebration not only is the mystery of Christ proclaimed by the ministry of the Church, but the work of salvation, the passing from spiritual death to life, is accomplished.

In baptism, and more especially in the Eucharist by com-

---

[10] Jerusalem Bible (London: Darton, Longman & Todd, 1966), Chronological Table, p. 456.

[11] L. Bouyer, op. cit., p. 21.

mon participation in the commemoration, by common participation in the body and blood of their crucified Lord, Christians become partakers of his cross. This gives a vital meaning to the words of Our Lord at the Last Supper: "This is my body which will be given for you; do this as a memorial of me" (Luke 22:19).

In the first centuries the commemoration of the death on the cross was celebrated in an especially solemn way every year.

By the fourth century the simple commemoration of the passion and death of Christ came to include the Holy Saturday vigil. By the fifth century, the Pasch came to refer only to Easter Sunday.

The Paschal vigil, which included the first Easter Mass and therefore was a bridge between the *triduum* commemorating the death of Our Lord and the Easter celebration of his glorious Resurrection, was the culmination of the whole liturgical year. The Sunday which began during the vigil with the Easter Mass was at once part of the *triduum* commemorating the passion and death of Our Lord and also the first day of the fifty days which continued the remembrance of the Resurrection right up to Pentecost. The *triduum* was a special time of penance and preparation for Easter. By the year 384, Lent was fixed at six weeks (it had been three weeks and also eight weeks), and Thursday, the beginning of the *triduum,* was the fortieth day of Lent, so that the *triduum* was regarded as a very special period added on to Lent.

But this was no mere service of commemoration. The Church, in celebrating "sacramentally" the mystery of salvation and the death and Resurrection of Christ, made real also the saving power of the death and Resurrection. This "realisation" was achieved in the two great sacraments which are essentially linked to the Paschal vigil: baptism, which applies the results of the passion and death of Christ to each individual baptised, and the Eucharist, which is the memorial of the sacrificial death and Resurrection of Christ—a sacrament which brings about what it signifies.

There is no better way of understanding the fundamental

importance given to baptism in the liturgy than by considering the ceremonies of the Paschal vigil which are, partly at
least, meaningless without their culmination in the giving of
baptism and the celebration of the Eucharist. Those who were
already baptised took part in the ceremonies in solidarity
with those about to be baptised, and also in commemoration
of their own baptism and as an opportunity for them to renew their own baptismal promises and their baptismal fer-
vor.

The rites of initiation *par excellence* to which all other
initiation rites had been a preparation was the feast of
Christ's death and Resurrection, the feast of the Pasch or
Passover, which in Christian usage we call Easter. As Bouyer
says:

> This simple statement sums up the whole economy of the
> revelation and development of the Word of God in Scripture
> and in the preaching of the Church.
>   What in fact is the Passover? First of all, it is the event that
> created people of God in the old covenant: God's basic inter-
> vention corresponding to the promise made to Abraham. God
> "passed" mysteriously through Egypt where his people were
> in bondage and enabled them to "pass" out of this bondage
> into freedom, out of the darkness of death into the light of
> life.
>   This double etymological interpretation of the word "Pass-
> over," in connection with the exodus of the Jews from Egypt,
> sums all the Jewish, and afterwards Christian tradition, recog-
> nised in the ancient Passover.[12]

The Paschal candle played a big part in this ceremony
commemorating passing from darkness to light.

The Paschal Candle

The ceremony began in complete darkness, symbolising
the darkness of sin and death, with the blessing of the
sacred fire intended for lighting the Paschal candle. The
light and the Paschal candle itself symbolised Christ, the
light of the world "who enlightens every man coming into

---

[12] L. Bouyer, *Christian Initiation* (London: Burns & Oates, 1960),
p. 81.

the world" but enlightens the baptised in a special way. So the light of the Paschal candle represents the "enlightenment" which was one of the names of baptism. The passing of this light to the members of the assembly by tapers lit at the Paschal candle shows how the Church spreads this light through its members and how they pass it on to others.

Then came the *Exsultet,* the great hymn of triumphal joy, the hymn in praise of the Paschal light which spreads through the world, which frees from the darkness of sin and which in baptism purifies and renews. In this hymn, the relationship, the continuity between the Old Testament Pasch and the Christian Paschal vigil is brought out. As Father O'Shea says:

> The passage of Christ from death to glorious life was prefigured by the passage of the Israelites through the Red Sea. Now Christ's passage is re-enacted in His Church through and by the sacraments celebrated on this night. The sacred mysteries of baptism and the Eucharist "separate believers in Christ from the vices of the world and the darkness of sin, restore them to grace and join them to holiness" (in the words of the *Exsultet*); Baptism ("the sanctification of this night") puts all evil to flight, washes away sins, restores innocence to the fallen and joy to those who mourn. On this night heaven is joined to earth and the divine to the human.[13]

The Readings

The readings are a summary of the way the light of salvation illuminated the history of Israel. (Whether there were twelve readings or not before the seventh century is not certain.) This light took its origin in the creation, which the Jews saw not as an event explaining the beginning of the world, but as the first event of salvation history. The creation itself is a type of baptism.

The account of the deluge was read as being another type of baptism. Just as the old wicked world of the time of Noah was buried in the waters of the deluge and a new regenerated world emerged after this burial by the waters, so the Chris-

[13] William J. O'Shea, *Sacraments of Initiation* (Englewood Cliffs, N.J.: Prentice-Hall, 1966), p. 23.

tian, by baptism, is regenerated by being buried in the waters of baptism and, through Christ's Resurrection, comes out of the waters to a new life.

The symbolism here was the destruction of sin and the beginning of a new world of grace.

The Exodus story occupied a central place in these readings because, as we have seen, it was the type, *par excellence,* of the passage from death to life which Christ had made and which by grace he enabled all baptised to make through this sacrament. The readings were interspersed with chants, and after the reading of the Exodus the Canticle of Moses was sung as a prophecy of the victory of Christ over death.

Other readings describe the sacrifice required of Abraham, as a prelude to the covenant between God and Abraham and his posterity, the renewal of the covenant between God (Yahweh) and his people, the reading from Isaiah about the remnant and the vineyard of Yahweh, and the account of the vision of the dry bones from Ezekiel 37:1–14. This vision, rather bizarre for modern readers, is full of symbolic instruction. It is a prophecy of the life-giving activity of the Holy Spirit in baptism and in the other sacraments of initiation.

The Blessing of the Baptismal Water (Blessing of the Font)

After the readings the catechumens were led to the pool, bath or font where they were to be baptised. The chant which the Church appoints for this procession is Psalm 42, its opening verse expressing the ardent desire for baptism in the hearts of the catechumens: "As a doe longs for running streams, so longs my soul for you, my God. My soul thirsts for God—the God of life." It stirs the desire for God, the desire to encounter and belong to Christ and his mystery. Bouyer says:

> In a sense it is the desire for death accepted without flinching, but the desire for Christ's kind of death, that is, death which will kill death as it has killed sin. So in the end it is the desire for life, super-abundant life, the life of the resurrection, life

that not only overcomes death but does away with it: life drawn from the living spring of the living God.[14]

The blessing of the baptismal water, the baptisms and the professional of baptismal faith were the highlights of the whole ceremony before the Easter Mass. The Mass itself was the other great feature of the Paschal night.

The prayer for the blessing of the water is very important because it contains doctrine about baptism.

The actual blessing is preceded by an introduction which refers to the spirit of God brooding over the waters of creation and likens this to the Spirit, who is ready to come to sanctify the baptismal water. The reference to the deluge in this introduction teaches us that baptism, awakening to the life of God men who were dead as the consequence of sin, was the point of departure for a new life.

The preface of the blessing of the water contains references to a whole list of events connected with water: the waters divided from the firmament (in Genesis 1:6), the four rivers which watered the Garden of Eden (Genesis 2:10), the water that Moses made spring from the rock (Exodus 17:6). Then there are some happenings associated with water which are mentioned in the New Testament—the miracle of Cana and the walking on the water. By his baptism in the Jordan, Christ sanctified the water, and the water and blood flowing from the side of Christ on the cross are the classical symbols of baptism and the Eucharist. The preface shows the two-fold element of exorcism and blessing. Before blessing, the water is subject to the devil as all creation. Exorcism is needed to drive out Satan. The blessing calls on the action of the Lord: "All powerful God, in your goodness, help us, . . . in your kindness breathe on and bless these waters with your mouth." It also includes a true epiclesis calling on the Holy Spirit to come: "May the power of the Holy Spirit come down on all that is within this fount. . . ."

During the blessing, the two candles which were used to give light to the celebrant were plunged into the baptismal

[14] L. Bouyer, *Christian Initiation,* p. 95.

water to symbolise the gift of the Holy Spirit, who descended in the form of fire. This Roman rite gave way several centuries later to the practice in certain Frankish churches of using the Paschal candle instead. This is the usage in our present rite. The meaning also changed, so that the rite symbolised Christ our light going down into the waters.

The custom of infusing chrism into the water was instituted very early in the Roman liturgy. The old books describe only the pouring of the holy chrism into the water. Later on it was seen to symbolise the Holy Spirit's descent on the waters at the beginning of creation to sanctify them.

The Biblical symbolism and the blessing affirm a double function of the baptismal water: it is a washing which purifies and at the same time it brings forth to new life.

After the blessing of the water the baptisms took place. It was for this purpose that the water was blessed, and in principle this was done only during the Paschal ritual. And it was natural and desirable that the blessing should be followed immediately by the baptisms, without which the whole of the liturgy of Holy Saturday night, of Lent, and of the octave of Pentecost loses much of its meaning. The Pasch of the Christian, his initiation, makes him a beneficiary of the Pasch of Christ. According to St Paul, baptism made the Christian die with Christ, made him participate in the mystery of Christ's burial and his descent to hell, and caused him to rise with Christ to live the life of heaven where Christ already is at the right hand of the Father. The celebration of baptisms, from the second century on, was reserved for Sunday, as it was a weekly "Paschal" day.

For many centuries, baptism was by immersion, though there were obviously certain exceptions to this rule, as in the case of the sick.

But this was not total immersion for adults. Total immersion only came later and was primarily for children, though in some places it was used also for adults, and it is still allowed in the present Code. The candidate normally stood up in the water up to his knees or waist while the one who baptised him either poured the water on his head or held his head under the water pouring from the spouts into the pool.

The candidate stripped before going into the pool. There were separate baptistries for men and women.

There was no pronouncing of the form at the same time as the pouring of the water, as is necessary for validity these days.

The profession of faith which the candidate made in answer to the three questions was itself the form. The candidate was immersed or had water poured on his head by the minister as he made his three-fold Trinitarian profession. The questions were the same as those asked now just *before* baptism, and they go back to the second century at least, for they are mentioned in St Hippolytus at the beginning of the third century.

The questions were (1) "(Name) Do you believe in God the Father Almighty, the Creator of heaven and earth? (2) (Name) Do you believe in Jesus Christ, His Son, Our Lord, who was born into this world to suffer for it? (3) (Name) Do you believe in the Holy Spirit, the Holy Catholic Church, the Communion of Saints, the Resurrection of the Flesh and life everlasting?" To each of these questions the answer is "I do believe."

The practice of three-fold immersion lasted longer than the interrogation for baptising. Baptism by infusion did not become general until the fifteenth century. The modern form of baptism—the priest pronouncing the words over the candidate—appears to have originated in Gaul, probably from emergency baptisms. What began as an emergency formula in time became the normal procedure, except for the solemn baptisms at Easter. It gradually came to be used at all times, because by then infant baptism was the rule and the declarative form "I baptise you" appears more natural for the baptism of infants than the ancient form. As Father O'Shea says,

It must be admitted that the ancient form had its advantages. It certainly expressed more clearly that baptism is an action that involves the candidate as well as the priest. Baptism clearly appeared as a personal action, a pact concluded between the Church and the candidate. The present formula suffers from the disadvantage of making the candidate seem passive in the very act of baptism.[15]

While the present form may be quite suitable for infant baptism, it is far from desirable in the case of adults and is just one more example of the difficulty of having a ritual which is adapted neither to infant nor to adult baptism.

St Cyril of Jerusalem gives an account of what happened at baptism.

Then you are led to the holy pool of divine baptism as Christ taken down from the Cross was laid in the tomb already prepared. Each one was questioned in the name of the Father and of the Son and of the Holy Spirit. You made the profession of salvation and you are plunged into the water three times and came forth, signifying Christ's burial for three days. *By this action you died and you were born* and the saving water was for you at once a grave and the womb of a mother.[16]

After this climax of the Paschal vigil, the newly baptised together with the faithful went on immediately to the Easter Mass, the celebration of the Eucharist, the memorial to Christ dead and risen from the dead. The celebration of the Eucharist on that special night referred not only to the personal triumph of Christ but to the individual Christian who, through baptism, had shared in that triumph.

THE EASTER MASS

The Mass was not only the supreme climax of the whole vigil but the completion of the baptismal rites as well. Many of the texts of this Mass refer to baptism. They presume that baptism has only just taken place; and so in the Epistle St Paul reminds each Christian that the mystery of Christ dead and risen from the dead is his own mystery too, that he is raised up with Christ. This unique mystery of Christ and the Christian is recalled in the Preface—"by His death He has

[15] O'Shea, *op. cit.*, p. 27.
[16] Lecture 20 on the Mysteries, quoted by O'Shea, *op. cit.*, p. 27.

destroyed our death and in rising again he has restored our life." The Mass is a joyful one. Not only because Christ is risen from the dead but also because the Alleluias of the Christian are his own special cry of triumph, which he gives now in rising from the tomb with Christ once and for all by his baptism and which he repeats every day by his participation in the Eucharist. The Collect prays that God will preserve in the new children of his family the spirit of the doctrine he has given them and that, renewed in body and spirit, they may accomplish sincerely their duties as Christians. The Epistle warns them, "Since you have been brought back to true life with Christ, you must look for the things that are in Heaven, where Christ is, sitting at God's right hand" (Colossians 3:1). The great Easter Alleluias are the songs of triumph of the Church. They express the joy of the Resurrection and the joy that belongs to all Christians because Christ's Resurrection has been made our own. The secret prayer relates also to baptism, for it asks that the sacrifice created by the Paschal mystery may be an eternal remedy for us.

The Paschal mystery of the death and Resurrection of Our Lord is the source of the Eucharistic sacrifice. We are incorporated into that same mystery by baptism. The fact that baptism was immediately followed by the celebration of the Eucharist in which baptism had given the new Christians the right to take full part, shows that the Eucharist can really be regarded as one of the sacraments of initiation. For many centuries it was joined closely with baptism, as a rite of initiation, as the introduction into divine mysteries which, as we have seen, is a characteristic of initiation rites in many other religions.

The new Christian's taking a new name when he came out of the water was a symbol of his new life in Christ. It recalls the changing of Saul's name to Paul. He was also given white garments in which his cleansed body was clad. During the whole of the Easter octave, from the celebration of their baptism until Low Sunday, those baptised on Easter Eve continued to wear these baptismal robes.

Each day during this week the neophytes took part in the

special celebrations of the Eucharist that were held in the stational churches of Rome. Because these Masses were proper to the feast and the season, they formed a prolonged contemplation of the whole mystery of Christ, the Paschal mystery, and consequently of the mystery of Christian initiation, the introduction into the Paschal mystery.

POST-BAPTISMAL ANOINTING

After baptism, the baptised were anointed with chrism. There is some confusion about this post-baptismal anointing and it was different in different places in the early centuries. In the early Church there was not so much thought given to separating the two sacraments of baptism and of confirmation and their effects.

In the Roman liturgy, at all events, there was from the time of Hippolytus an anointing after baptism, and this was applied to baptism (i.e., not regarded as part of confirmation). In the middle of the fifth century the Council of Orange (441) made it clear that an anointing, belonging to baptism and given after baptism, formed one with the rite of immersion and completed it symbolically.

The chrism used in the anointing was always blessed by the bishop; the oil of catechumens, however, could be blessed by a priest. At Rome, the blessing of the chrism took place at the Pope's Mass on Holy Thursday between his Communion and that of the people. The blessing was very simple. It was given by a triple breathing (exsufflation) on the oil, with which balsam had already been mixed. Then the consecrating prayer, which is still in use, was said.

THE SYMBOLISM OF THE ANOINTING ACCORDING TO THE PRAYERS OF THE BLESSING OF THE CHRISM

It is necessary to know the preface to the actual Mass of the blessing of the chrism and the consecrating prayer of the chrism in order to understand the meaning of the post-baptismal anointing. First of all, according to these texts, the

anointing is destined to express the positive effect of the
sacrament of baptism—sanctification—while these prayers
attribute to the water the negative effect—the remission of
sins. And so according to the preface of the Mass, the water
destroys the corruption which man had contracted by his
first birth, while the chrism makes the baptised person pleasing to God.[17]

The consecrating prayer presents in the same way the
effects proper to each of the two rites of baptism. Just as at
the deluge, a figure of baptism, the pouring of the water
purified the world from sin while the olive branch brought
back by the dove signified the return of peace, in the same
way Christian baptismal waters wash away sins and the
anointing with oil brings peace and joy.

Another essential element of the symbolism which can be
discerned in the formulary is that the anointing makes the
Christian configured to Christ. In this way we come back
again to the teaching of St Paul (Romans 8:29) but by
means of the Biblical theme of anointing, which is so frequent in the first apostolic catechesis.

In the Old Testament, indeed, oil was used to anoint
priests, kings and prophets. The anointing was a figure of
the anointing of Christ, whose name means "the anointed
one." With the anointing of Jesus, the prayer insists, oil has
been raised to a dignity which it never had before, even when
it was used to consecrate Aaron. The same text relates this
consecration of Christ to the coming of the Holy Spirit on
him on the day of his baptism and gives a special emphasis
to his royal character: the accomplishment of the prophecy
which announced the anointing of the Messiah as King
(Psalm 44:8).

The post-baptismal anointing signifies that the Christian
shares in the spiritual anointing which Christ received at his
baptism. This idea is in keeping with the constant tradition
of the Fathers. Being conformed to Christ, the one who is
anointed participates in the royal priesthood (I Peter 2:9;
Apocalypse 5:9–10) and also in the prophetic role of Jesus.
And so the preface of the Mass of the chrism shows the oil

[17] See Béraudy, op. cit., p. 551.

as the ornament of those who have been raised to the royal priestly and prophetic dignity. The consecrating prayer emphasises also that the anointing makes those who are baptised participants of heavenly glory and of life eternal—the two blessings which, according to the New Testament, are given in Christ (II Timothy 2:20; Romans 6:23; I John 1:2; 5:11; 12:20; I Peter 3:22).

So the baptised person becomes, through the anointing, a new man, immortal and incorruptible, of whom St Paul speaks (Ephesians 4:22–24; Colossians 3:9–10; I Corinthians 15:53). According to the preface of the Mass, the anointing with chrism itself is a symbol of a garment of incorruptibility and immortality.[18]

THE WHITE GARMENT

The neophyte, who had taken off his old garments before going down into the bath, put on the new and white garments when he emerged from the bath. By this rite the Church signified to him that he had changed the garment of corruptibility and was now clothed with glory. The colour white, indeed, showed that the Christian was participating already in the glory of the Resurrection. In the Bible white is the colour of the garments of God himself (Daniel 7:9), of Christ on the day of the Transfiguration, when he showed the glory of his Resurrection, of the eighty ancients in the sky (Apocalypse 4:4), and of the countless number of the elect (Apocalypse 7:9–13). White is also the colour of the robes with which one must be clothed in order to take part in the banquet of the heavenly spouse, namely the Eucharist. From another point of view, these garments recall the symbolic veil with which the priests of the Old Testament always covered their heads. In this way the garments show the priestly character of the baptised person.[19]

It is very easy but also important to realise that initiation was not just a baptising, it was a whole complex of ceremonies and rites, from the first ceremonies at the entry of

[18] Beraudy, *op. cit.*, pp. 560–61.
[19] *Ibid.*, p. 562.

the catechumenate right up to the moment when the candidates were baptised with the newly blessed baptismal water. We have been brought up with a legalistic attitude to the sacraments. Our instruction has stressed what constitutes the absolute minimum for baptism, with regard both to disposition and to rites. At the same time the overriding importance of baptism for salvation was emphasised, so that often the main thing one learned was the minimum emergency baptism which anyone might suddenly be faced with the necessity of giving.

It is true that it is necessary for purposes of theological accuracy to distinguish between what is essential and what is nonessential. It is also necessary to know how to baptise in case of necessity. But as we have seen, if one were to restrict baptism to the central rite of actual baptising, this would impoverish the whole sacrament. The rites which surround baptism and which in the olden days covered a very long period were all sacramental rites, what we would call sacramentals. Each in its own way led up to, and showed the meaning of, the central essential rite, and shared in the dignity and sacramentality of baptism. In other words, it is artificial to separate in the liturgy the essence of the sacrament from those rites which are nonessential but which are rich in instruction and meaning.

By the fifth century, as we have seen, baptism was part of the vast complex of sacred rites which led up to it, commented upon its actual celebration and prolonged that celebration.

THE MINISTER OF BAPTISM

The usual minister of baptism was the bishop. Of course, the bishop did not baptise all the candidates himself, but he presided at the assembly of initiation and performed certain ceremonies that were reserved for him. The creation of rural parishes brought up the question of what exactly were the prerogatives of the bishop, especially with regard to the post-baptismal anointing. After a period of uncertainty, to which conciliar texts give witness, the consecration of chrism everywhere was reserved to the bishop. At Rome, the priest or the deacon who baptised needed the authorisation of the bishop and used chrism which had been blessed by him. This discipline remains in force to the present day. In order to consecrate baptismal water and to anoint those who are baptised, priests and deacons must use the chrism prepared by the bishop. Moreover, the baptism of adults is normally reserved to the ordinary of the faithful, who can, and of course does, delegate his power. In this way the Church wishes to stress that the priest who baptises does not act as head of the community itself but only as assistant to the bishop who is the principle of all life in the Church.

THE GODPARENT

The Role of "Guarantor" before the Sixth Century

In the ancient discipline of the catechumenate each candidate who was presented for baptism was accompanied by a guarantor. The first time that the guarantor took part was in the ceremony of admission to the catechumenate, when he gave witness to the manner of life of the catechumen. During the whole time of preparation for baptism he helped the person to be baptised in his efforts to adhere to the faith and to adopt a pattern of Christian conduct. Finally, at the ceremony of the inscribing of the name he gave a guarantee of the conduct of the person who had been entrusted to him.

Children were normally presented and brought to baptism by their own parents, although sometimes this role was taken on by others; for example, a master would present his slaves. The one who brought the children to baptism was asked to renounce Satan and to profess the faith in the name of those to be baptised.

The Role of Godparents after the Sixth Century

When baptism was mainly of children—after the sixth century—the role of godparents changed. Obviously they did not have to prepare the candidate for baptism and the profession of faith, but they had to see to it that after the children had been initiated, they passed, when they grew up, from a passive life to an active life according to God.

At Rome, the godparent took part in the prebaptismal ceremonies. In the rite of the inscription of the name he did this on behalf of his godchild. During the scrutinies, he signed the godchild with the sign of the cross. The godparent also had the role of renouncing Satan before baptism and professing the faith in the name of the candidate. And he also took the godchild in his hands after the post-baptismal anointing with chrism.

St Caesarius explained that by taking part in all these ceremonies the godparents were taking on the duty of guarantor of the faith of the infant, so that it was their duty to see to the Christian education of their godchild by their example and by their exhortations. In doing this, the godparents were not interfering with the role of the parents. Parents, indeed, were bound to obtain a Christian education for their children when they agreed to their baptism, and this consent was always required before the Church would accept an infant for baptism, except in exceptional cases such as danger of death. Nevertheless, in the education of the baptised child the godparent had a very special role. Indeed, he was regarded as the representative of the Church, which also had agreed to the baptism and which by this fact had taken on —as a parent in a natural family does for the natural life of the child—the responsibility for the faith and supernatural life of the baptised child.[20]

FURTHER DEVELOPMENTS IN THE RITE OF BAPTISM

At the beginning of the sixth century the catechumenate disappeared. Since Roman society had now become profoundly influenced by Christianity, the catechumenate was no longer necessary. The ancient rites of entry to the catechumenate and the inscription of the name of the person to be baptised were combined with the first scrutiny. On that oc-

[20] Béraudy, *op. cit.*, pp. 562–564.

casion the ceremony of bathing, the exsufflation, the imposing of the sign of the cross and the giving of blessed salt took place, and the whole ceremony closed with the exorcisms over the chosen ones.

The second scrutiny remained the same. But the third scrutiny, in addition to the giving of the Creed, included the giving of the Lord's Prayer and of the Gospels. This occurred about 550. At the same time the Nicene Creed took the place of the Apostles creed. By this time the prebaptismal customs were being revised with infant baptism in mind.

BAPTISM AT ROME FROM THE SIXTH TO THE NINTH CENTURIES

From the sixth century onwards, baptism was, in the usual course of events, infant baptism. The ritual was adjusted to allow for this change of custom.

It was natural that when the person to be baptised was an adult, he would play an active role. As we have seen, this was such an active role indeed that, especially in the very act of baptism, it seemed almost as if the person being baptised was acting as partial minister of the sacrament. The Fathers even discussed whether infant baptism was valid because small children were not capable of professing their faith, which was regarded as one of the essential elements in the sacrament.

St Augustine settled the question once and for all in a famous passage in one of his sermons: "Mother Church lends the feet of others to babies so that they can come, the hearts of others so that they may believe, the tongues of others so that they may profess their faith." [21]

Infant baptism was officially accepted by the Church at the Council of Carthage, which was approved by Pope Zozimus. The Council of Trent gives testimony to this belief of the Church: *middle 16th century*

> If anyone says that infants recently born, even though they are born of baptised parents, should not be baptised, or says that they do not derive original sin from Adam which must

[21] Sermon 176, quoted by Béraudy, *op. cit.*, p. 538.

be remitted by the laver of regeneration for the attainment of eternal life, and that consequently the words "baptism in remission of sin" are in their case not true but false, let him be anathema. For the Apostle's words "by one man sin entered into this world, and by sin death, and so death passed upon all men in whom all have sinned" (Romans 5:12) must not be understood except as the Catholic Church throughout the world has always understood them. It is because of the rule of faith, received from the Apostles, that even infants who have not yet been able to commit any personal sin, are truly baptised in remission of sin, and that that is cleansed in them which they derived from their birth. "Unless a man be born again of water and the Holy Ghost he cannot enter into the kingdom of God." [22]

The Council of Trent is reiterating here almost verbatim what the Council of Carthage said.

But because of the prevalence of infant baptisms; the rite of baptism was changed. The role of the recipient was reduced to a purely passive one. The interrogation about the faith were put before the actual baptism, and during the baptism itself a formula pronounced by the minister alone was substituted for the former interrogative form. This change probably did not become common before the seventh century.

The fact of infant baptism was responsible for joining the handing over of the Gospels to that of the Creed and the Our Father, and this replaced the old instructions of the catechumenate, which no longer were of any practical value because the subjects for baptism were children.

The scrutinies, on the other hand, were increased. In the second half of the sixth century they were increased to seven as if to make up by an increase of divine intervention for the lack of activity of the recipients and to show that in this preparation everything is the work of grace. Their number was raised to seven, counting the one on Holy Saturday. There was no need for the other scrutinies to be celebrated with Mass on Sundays before the whole Christian assembly, because they had lost much of their importance now that they were directed only to little children.

[22] Denziger 791; quoted by Bernard Leeming, S.J., *Principles of Sacramental Theology* (2d. ed.; London: Longman's, 1966), pp. 76–77.

The Sacramentary of Adrian contains an ordo (or ritual) for preparation for baptism which is not earlier than the seventh century. This ordo contained only two assemblies preparatory to baptism apart from the prebaptismal ceremonies of Holy Saturday—namely, the giving of the salt followed by the prayer Omnipotes and the handing over of the Gospels (which was the only one of the three "handing over" rites that required no response from the recipient).

HISTORY OF THE PRESENT BAPTISMAL RITUAL

The Roman ritual that is still in force was first issued by Pope Paul V in 1614. The part in it concerning baptism was based on the Liber Sacerdotalis, a collection of rites made by Albert Castellani, OP, in 1523.

A bull issued by Leo X in 1520 had imposed this book on the Latin Church, but the Pope died before the book was actually published and the bull did not take effect. Castellani drew up two alternative rituals for baptism, both of which he intended for infant baptism. The prayers and ceremonies were taken from earlier sources, and most of the texts used are from the Gelasian Sacramentary which takes us back to the fifth and sixth centuries. The texts from these sources were written originally for adults. Although the Church has adapted the rites for infants, she has never composed special texts for them. The Roman ritual took over two formularies of Castellani with but slight modifications, but designated the first, shorter ritual for the baptism of infants and made the second, longer one the rite for the baptism of adults.

COMMENTARY ON THE PRESENT BAPTISMAL RITUAL

Prebaptismal Rites

The prebaptismal rites are those during which the celebrant wears purple vestments, that is, those which come before the profession of faith and the actual baptism in the Roman ritual.

They correspond to the ancient discipline of catechumens, and so in order to understand their meaning we must first put them in their historical context. But the comparison of the present with the past raises a problem, both in the case of adults and in the case of children.

For adults, the catechumenate is reduced nowadays to a series of instructions, mostly of an intellectual nature, given before baptism. In comparison with the ancient discipline, the present arrangement leaves too much to the candidates themselves. On the path towards baptism they no longer have the benefit of the sacramentals, which in former days assured the catechumens of the support of the Church and help from God, without which man cannot take the slightest step in the work of salvation. It is on this account, to make up for this deficiency at least in a partial way, that missionaries have introduced stages in the preparation for baptism, with additional rites including apologetics. Nowadays, the adult baptisms are so numerous in missionary countries as well as in the great cities of our older Christian countries, that we should hope the Church will give these authentic liturgical rites their traditional place and thus their full spiritual efficacy. Indeed, the Vatican Council makes provision for such a restoration. This point will be dealt with at greater length in the second half of this book, where some actual innovations will be mentioned.

In the case of infants, whose role in baptism is purely passive, a stage of preliminary formation obviously cannot take place. The Church assures the exercise of their life of faith by instruction after baptism when they come of age and are able to profit from it, and so she has organised a whole post-baptismal discipline which replaces the old custom of the catechumenate. In this discipline the intervention of God is manifested by the sacraments of confirmation and Holy Eucharist, and also by the sacrament of penance, while catechesis is given by the Church and by the family with the object, not only of instructing a child in the faith, but also of helping him to learn to live as a true believer should. In countries such as England, where religious instruction is allowed in public schools, the teachers supplement the work of parents and priests. In countries such as the United States, voluntary catechists form a network of religious instructors with the same role, for children in public schools. This brings in the whole question of the catechetical renewal, which will also be treated in the second half of the book.

The retention of the prebaptismal rites in the present ritual should not, however, be considered an anachronism. The presence of exorcisms, for example, is easily justified for infants as well as adults, because they both need to be delivered from subjection to Satan and his influence. Moreover, these different rites stress the road which all must take in order to respond to the grace of God. For adults this response is required before baptism; for children it is part of the commitments which have been undertaken for them in baptism.

First Part of the Baptismal Ritual

The questions. The opening questions to the godparents— "What do you ask of the Church of God?" and "What does faith offer you?"—recall the rites which, as we have already seen, were used in the early Church for admission to the long catechumenate: they are the remainder of the preliminary enquiry and instruction in the rudiments of the faith. The three-fold ritual—breathing on the face of the child with the exorcism, making the sign of the Cross on the forehead and breast, and the laying on of hands as a mark of blessing and protection—dates back to early times.

The prayer Omnipotens. The ancient prayer *Omnipotens* accompanies the laying on of hands and also refers to the entry into the catechumenate:

Almighty, everlasting God, Father of our Lord Jesus Christ, look upon this thy servant, whom thou has called to the first lessons of the Faith. Drive out of him all blindness of heart; break the bonds of Satan which have bound him. Open to him, O Lord, the door of thy mercy. Steeped in this symbol of thy wisdom may he no longer be tainted with evil desires, but rather spread about him the fragrance of thy commandments, as he serves thee happily in thy Church and grows holier with each passing day. Through the same Christ our Lord. Amen.

The prayer *Omnipotens* stresses that God enters into a new relationship with man from the time that he receives the very first announcement of the message of salvation, the rudiments of faith. On the one hand, the links binding man to Satan are denounced: "Break all the bonds with which Satan has bound him." On the other hand, the catechumen is already the object of divine mercy: "Open to him the door of your mercy"; he is also bound to the Church, in which from now on he will serve God: "that he should serve you in the Church." The divine protection and kindness in his regard will be further expressed by the gift of salt ("the sign of your wisdom").

Preces nostras. The sign of the cross traced on the catechumen is commented on by the prayer *Preces nostras,* also of great antiquity:

Hear our prayer, Lord God, and guard this chosen servant. May thy strength never fail him now, for we have traced upon him the sign of Christ's cross. May he always remember what he learns of thy greatness and thy glory. May he keep thy commandments and be worthy, too, to have glory, the glory of new life in thee. Through Christ our Lord. Amen.

The sign of the cross protects him with the power which enables him to keep "the first elements of greatness and glory."

The blessing and giving of salt. The blessing of the salt and its symbolism are explained by the prayer with which it is blessed:

I adjure thee in the name of God the Father almighty, in the love of Jesus Christ our Lord, in the power of the Holy Spirit. I adjure thee through the living, true and Holy God, the God who made thee for the well-being of the human race, and commanded thee to be hallowed by his servants for the use of those who come to the knowledge of him by faith. In the name of the Holy Trinity, through thee may Satan be put to flight. Wherefore, O Lord God, we beseech thee, sanctify this salt and bless it; and make of it a sovereign remedy to linger within the inmost being of all who partake of it. In the name of that same Lord Jesus Christ, who is to come to judge the living and the dead and the world by fire. Amen.

A little of the salt is placed in the mouth of the child and the minister says: "(Name) Receive this salt, learning from it how to relish what is right and good. May it make your way easy to eternal life. Amen."

The blessed salt which in its human use serves to keep things from decay will through its blessing preserve the catechumen from the corruptions of his passions and from Satan, who is the father of them: "May the salt become the sacrament of salvation which will drive away the enemy."

In addition to being regarded as perfect medicine, there are other meanings given to the salt in the liturgy. It is considered, in rather a forced way, as the first food given to the catechumen while he waits patiently for the perfect food, the Eucharist. A more natural meaning is based on the idea that just as salt gives flavour to food and preserves it, so salt is a symbol of the wisdom coming down from God, and this meaning is probably a reference to our Lord's words: "You are the salt of the earth."

The first part of the baptismal rite ends with the prayer *Deus Patrum Nostrum:*

> God of our Fathers, O God with whom all truth begins, look upon thy servant who now has tasted salt as the first nourishment at thy table. Do not leave him hungry. Give to his soul food in abundance that he may be eager, hopeful and lighthearted in the service of thy Name. Lead him we pray thee, to the waters of new life, that, with all who are faithful to thee, he may merit the eternal rewards thou hast promised. Through Christ our Lord. Amen.

This prayer, as we have seen, is also of ancient origin.

Second Part of the Baptismal Ritual

The second part of the rite of infant baptism—and therefore of our ritual—has retained very little from ancient times. Of the original six scrutinies, one exorcism alone has been kept.

I adjure thee, unclean spirit, in the name of the Father and of the Son and of the Holy Ghost to depart and remain far away from this servant of God. He commands thee now who walked dry-shod upon the waters, and when Peter would have perished in the sea stretched out to him his saving hand. And so, accursed spirit, give heed to the sentence passed upon thee. Give honour to the living and true God, give honour to Jesus Christ his Son, and to the Holy Ghost, and begone from this servant of God; for God and our Lord Jesus Christ in his goodness has called him to his holy grace and blessing and to the waters of baptism.

The signing of the forehead with the cross and the imposition of hands have also remained: During the signing the priest says: "And this sign of the Cross which we put upon his forehead, do thou foul spirit never dare to violate through the same Christ Our Lord." Then he places his hand upon the child's head with these words:

Holy Lord and Father, almighty and eternal God, author of light and of truth, we ask thy never-failing and kind fatherly love for this thy servant. Enlighten him in thy goodness with the light of thy own understanding. Cleanse him and sanctify him; give him true knowledge; that made worthy by the grace of thy Baptism he may be endowed with unwavering hope, sound judgment and a firm grasp of holy doctrine. Through Christ our Lord. Amen.

The ceremonies of exorcism may seem rather out of place with regard to children. But these rites refer to the fact that until baptism the soul of the child is in an unredeemed state, as part of the unredeemed world and is therefore to be regarder as subject to Satan. In the child's case this is a negative thing (not a positive thing obviously like possession) and is due to lack of grace, which Christ gained in rescuing mankind from the domination of the devil and which the child has not yet received.

The exorcisms as originally used in adult baptism were intended to help the adult convert in his struggle with evil before baptism, and of course that meaning still holds good when an adult is baptised with this ritual. Now they refer to the struggle against evil to which baptism commits the child and which the child will have to wage when he grows up.

The priest then leads the infant into church (the previous ceremonies should have taken place outside the church proper, e.g., in the porch or sacristy), saying, "Come into the temple of God, that your lot may be with Christ in life eternal."

This rite is a late addition coming from the thirteenth century. It does not make much sense at this point. In the early Church, once a person was a catechumen he could take some part in the services in the church, but only baptism gave full membership in the worshipping community. To put the symbolic entry into the Church in the middle of the preparatory rites is to deprive it of any clear meaning. It could perhaps be moved to the end of the first part of the rite, which corresponds to the making of a catechumen.[23]

The next set of ceremonies before the actual baptism recalls the ceremonies which in ancient times took place on Holy Saturday. The reciting of the Creed and the Our Father are really the old ceremony of "giving back" the Creed and the Lord's Prayer and the Gospels (to which there is now no reference).

Then comes a final exorcism before the entrance into the baptistry.

> I adjure you, each and every unclean spirit, in the name of God the Father almighty, in the name of Jesus Christ his Son, our Lord and our Judge, and by the power of the Holy Spirit, to be gone from this image of God, whom our Lord in his goodness has called to his holy temple that he himself may become a temple of the living God and the Holy Ghost may dwell in him. Through the same Christ our Lord, who will come to judge the living and the dead and the world by fire. Amen.

After this, the priest touches the ears and the nostrils of the child with his thumb moistened with saliva (though this is no longer obligatory) and using the word hallowed by Our Lord, "Ephpheta," which means "be you opened." As he anoints the nostrils he says, "To the sweet fragrance about you. As for thee, evil spirit, get thee gone, for God's judgement is

[23] See Charles Davis, *The Making of a Christian* (London and New York: Sheed & Ward, 1964), pp. 72–73.

upon thee." This anointing was, in fact, originally done with oil.

Then comes the hallowed custom of the renunciation of Satan, which, pronounced by the godparents on behalf of the children who cannot do this for themselves, has lost the dramatic force it had in the early Church.

There follows the anointing with the oil of catechumens upon the breast and between the shoulders, as the priest says, "I annoint you with this saving oil in Jesus Christ Our Lord, that you may have eternal life."

The meaning of the anointing with oil is to be found in the prayer *Deus Incrementorum,* with which the oil is blessed on Holy Thursday.

Third Part of the Baptismal Ritual

The actual baptism takes place after the anointing. It is preceded by a three-fold profession of faith in the form of question and answer, which as we have seen originally was an essential part of the actual baptismal form—indeed it *was* the baptismal form. In the baptism of infants, answers are given by the godparents.

The questions and answers are the following.

Do you believe in God the Father almighty, Creator of Heaven and Earth?
I do believe.
Do you believe in Jesus Christ his only Son, Our Lord, who was born in this world and who suffered for us?
I do believe.
Do you believe in the Holy Ghost, the Holy Catholic Church, the communion of Saints, the forgiveness of sins, the resurrection of the body and life everlasting?
I do believe.

The baptism itself is an example of how the Church can and does change the essential form. Now the form is said by the priest—"I baptise thee in the name of the Father and of the Son and the Holy Spirit"—as he pours water three times over the head of the child in the form of a cross.

The anointing with chrism takes place immediately after

the baptism. The priest says, while he makes the sign of the cross with the oil on the crown of the child's head:

> May Almighty God, the Father of our Lord Jesus Christ, who has given you new life through water and the Holy Ghost, and forgiven you all your sins himself anoint you with saving chrism in the same Jesus Christ our Lord, that you may have eternal life.

The imposing of the white garment and the giving of lighted candles have already been explained. The following words accompany these rites:

> Take this white garment, and see that you carry it without stain before the judgement seat of your Lord Jesus Christ, that you may have eternal life.

> Take this burning light and keep true to your baptism throughout a blameless life. Keep the commandments of God; that when the Lord shall come like a bridegroom to his marriage feast you, in company with all the saints, may meet him in the heavenly courts, and there live for ever.

This analysis of the present ritual and the way it has developed gives point to the efforts which are being made to adapt the baptismal rites (1) to make them more suitable for adults and infants as the decree on the liturgy demands, and (2) to make them more suitable for our modern circumstances.

Much has been done already to make baptism more meaningful. The use of the vernacular is a big step forward.

Another important step was the revival of the Easter vigil. Baptism is allowed or rather encouraged to be given during the vigil, and the ceremonies that come before the profession of faith are to be used.

The ritual for a new arrangement of ceremonies for adult baptism was issued by a decree on 16th April, 1962.

This divides the prebaptismal rites into six stages, baptism itself forming the seventh stage. In this way, the prebaptismal ceremonies can go along with the instruction in the faith. This is especially useful in pagan countries which, in some way, reproduce the circumstances that prevailed when these ceremonies were first instituted. The use of this ritual

is at the discretion of local ordinaries and some have chosen
to introduce a meaningful ritual of baptismal ceremonies—
some adapted from local religious customs—which are very
interesting and to which we refer in the second half of the
book.

CHAPTER IV

CONFIRMATION

The rites of initiation were so closely bound together in one whole ceremony in the early Church that it is very difficult in the first centuries to distinguish between baptism and confirmation.

In the East some theologians think that the two sacraments were conferred by the same set of ceremonies.

Historical research and theological interpretation are by no means finished tasks. Nevertheless, by restricting ourselves to Western and especially Roman liturgies, we can get a fair idea (1) of the fact that two distinct sacraments have always existed, (2) of the general development up to our own day of the rites of each, and (3) of the specific effects of each.

But in doing this we must beware of a legalistic separation of what really is and should be regarded as a whole.

As Father O'Shea says,

> The second stage of Christian initiation is the sacrament of confirmation. This is the sacred rite which, by the anointing with Chrism and the words of the bishop, bestows the Holy Spirit in a special way upon the baptised Christian. It equips the believer to live the Christian life more perfectly and to take his rightful part in the work of the Church. Confirmation is the complement and completion of baptism and can be rightly understood only in relation to that sacrament. Although confirmation is a separate sacrament, it nevertheless is not *isolated*. It stands in very close relationship to baptism and the Eucharist, being part of the single process of Christian initiation.[1]

It was, of course, far easier for the early Christians to realise this than it is for us, now that confirmation often

[1] William J. O'Shea, *Sacraments of Initiation* (Englewood Cliffs, N.J.: Prentice-Hall, 1966), pp. 47–48.

takes place years after baptism and the Eucharist may be received before confirmation.

Confirmation is the giving and receiving of the Holy Spirit, the third person of the blessed Trinity. This gift was received directly by the apostles and disciples on the first feast of Pentecost. But this gift was not intended for them alone. The Messianic prophecy most relevant here is the prophecy which Peter himself quoted in his sermon at nine o'clock on Pentecost morning to the Jerusalem crowd:

> This is what was foretold by the prophet Joel: In the last times,[2] God says, I will pour out my spirit upon all mankind, and your sons and daughters will be prophets. Your young men shall see visions, and your old men shall dream dreams; and I will pour out my spirit in those days upon my servants and hand-maids, so that they will prophesy.[3]

The gift of the Spirit was to be for all, but obviously all would not receive the Spirit in the miraculous way the first apostles and disciples did.

St Peter says in the same sermon that his hearers should be baptised; they will have their sins forgiven, *and then* they will receive the gift of the Spirit. And he adds, "This promise is for you and for your children, and for all those, however far away, whom the Lord our God calls to himself" (Acts 2:39).

However, it would be too much to read into this text a separate giving of the Spirit, distinct from baptism (which in the Bible and in tradition is also associated with the gift of the Spirit), unless we relate this text with the two classic confirmation texts also in the Acts. These two texts show clearly a rite after and in addition to baptism: the special gift of the Spirit by the imposition of hands.

The first is the clearer and more important witness to the existence of an independent rite distinct from baptism for giving the Holy Spirit; it is the only completely conclusive proof. It refers to the preaching of the deacon Philip in Samaria.

[2] A biblical expression meaning the Messianic times.
[3] Acts 2:17–18. The word "prophesy" does not necessarily mean to foretell the future but to bear witness, e.g. by martyrdom.

> When the apostles in Jerusalem heard that Samaria had accepted the word of God, they sent Peter and John to them, and they went down there, and prayed for the Samaritans to receive the Holy Spirit, for as yet he had not come down on any of them: they had only been baptised in the name of the Lord Jesus. Then they laid hands on them, and they received the Holy Spirit (Acts 8:14–17).

The clear conclusion is that Philip baptised, but a visit from the apostles at Jerusalem was necessary for the additional rite: the special giving of the Spirit.

The second passage is not quite so clear, but taken in conjunction with Acts 8:14–17, it seems to refer to a special giving of the Holy Spirit. It relates how (in Acts 19:1–7) Paul came across a group of disciples at Ephesus who had received only the baptism of John and had not even heard of the Holy Spirit. After instructing them and showing them that Jesus was the Messiah of whom John the Baptist was the herald, Paul baptised them "in the name of the Lord Jesus": and when Paul laid his hands upon them "the Holy Spirit came down upon them and they began to speak with tongues and to prophesy." The Holy Spirit was therefore given by the laying on of hands and the effects were similar to those experienced on the day of Pentecost.

Father O'Shea has listed a number of passages in the epistles which give confirmative evidence of the existence of a special rite which conferred the Holy Spirit.

> The love of God has been spread abroad in our hearts through the Holy Ghost that was given to us (Rom. 5:5). We received . . . the spirit which is of God (I Cor. 2:12). We were all made to drink of one spirit (I Cor. 12:13). God sent forth the spirit of his son into our hearts crying Abba—Father (Gal. 4:6). He that anointed us is God, who also sealed us and gave us the earnest [the pledge] of the Spirit in our hearts (II Cor. 1:21ff). In whom having also believed you were sealed with the Holy Spirit of promise (Eph. 1:13). Grieve not the Holy Spirit of God in whom you were sealed unto the day of redemption (Eph. 4:30). He saved us through the washing of regeneration and renewal of the Holy Spirit (Tit. 3:5). The anointing which you received of him abides in you (I Jn. 2:27). For it is impossible to restore again to repentence those who have once been enlightened, who have tasted the heavenly

gift, and have become partakers of the Holy Spirit and have tasted the goodness of the word of God and the powers of the age to come if they then commit apostasy (Heb. 6:4f).[4]

These passages must also be taken together with the fact that the writer Tertullian, whose testimony goes back in all probability to the early part of the second century, refers to a laying on of hands which gives the Holy Spirit; St Cyprian makes a similar reference. Confirmation was not seriously questioned as a sacrament until the Reformation. Some modern Anglicans regard confirmation as a sacrament in the full sense of the word and give it a very honoured position much more similar to that of the early Church than does the Catholic practice; the Anglicans make it a solemn affirmation of membership in the Church and a condition of taking Holy Communion.

HISTORY OF THE RITE

Confirmation at Rome until Fifth Century

In the very early centuries the two rites of initiation merged into one and the word "baptism" was used for the ceremony at which both sacraments were given.

The apostles Peter and John, according to the Acts, used a very simple ritual: "They prayed for the Samaritans to receive the Holy Spirit . . . then they laid hands on them, and they received the Holy Spirit" (Acts 8:14–17).

In North Africa, a little more than a century after, Tertullian describes the same ritual: "The hand is imposed in blessing calling and inviting the Holy Spirit."

In the third century, St Cyprian, Bishop of Carthage, gives a slightly more detailed description: "The newly-baptised person is presented to the head of the Church; he receives the Holy Spirit through our prayer and the imposition of our hand and is perfected by means of the Lord's sign (the sign of the cross)."

One may note here that some writers do not accept the

[4] O'Shea, op. cit., p. 55.

signing with the cross as a physical signing but as a spiritual effect which the Holy Spirit works in man.

At all events, the Roman liturgy has the clearest indication of two distinct rites for baptism and confirmation. At Rome there were two post-baptismal anointings. One remained linked to baptism, the other became attached to confirmation. The rite of confirmation was then formed round the imposition of hands and the anointing.

The *Apostolic Tradition* of Hippolytus in the third century, which gives the first known ritual at Rome, has reference to confirmation. Anointing with oil was part of the post-baptismal ceremonies from the middle of the second century onwards (as Tertullian witnesses), but in the rites outside Rome this anointing was connected with baptism, not confirmation, as the Council of Orange (441) later affirmed.

The *Apostolic Tradition* contained the following rites:

1. An imposition of the hands during the recitation of a petitionary formula which begged God to send the Holy Spirit and his grace on the newly baptised. This imposition of hands was a collective one, or at least there is no evidence that the prayer which accompanied it was not intended for all of those being confirmed.

2. The anointing of the head of the confirmed person with the oil of thanksgiving—chrism. During the anointing the minister said: "I anoint you with the holy oil in the Lord, the Father Almighty, Christ Jesus and the Holy Spirit."

3. The signing of the forehead.

4. The kiss of peace, with the formula: "The Lord be with you."

Confirmation from the Fifth to the Eighth Century

There are a number of documents for this period which give us information about the liturgy of confirmation at Rome. Besides several reference by ecclesiastical writers, we have the *Gelasian Sacramentary,* that of Adrian, and others. From the examination of all these documents it seems that the rite in use in Rome in the fifth century was very similar to that described by Hippolytus. The collective imposition of hands was still in use, but the formula said during this imposition had developed. From this time onwards, it mentioned the seven gifts of the Holy Spirit taken from liturgies outside Rome. This addition goes back at least to the fourth century, because it was witnessed by the Pope Siricius (384–399 A.D.).

The anointing and separate signing of the forehead were combined to become an anointing of the forehead in the form of the cross. This development also took place quite early, from the fifth century, according to Pope Innocent I. During the anointing, the bishop pronounced the formula: "The sign of Christ for eternal life" (according to the Gelasian ritual). The kiss of peace closed the ceremony, as in the times of Hippolytus.

The Organisation of the Ritual of Confirmation apart from Baptism

From the ninth century onwards, the administration of confirmation was often separated from that of baptism, and so the old Roman ordo of confirmation was filled out by the additional ceremony of entrance and of closing. These additions were made by having recourse mainly to Biblical verses that served to evoke the grace of the sacrament. From the time of the Pontifical of William Durand one of these verses served as a final blessing. The most important of all these additions was the prayer *Deus, qui apostolis tuis*.[5] This was relatively ancient, having already appeared at the time of Charlemagne; it came into the Roman liturgy by way of a liturgical book called the *Ordo Romanus Antiquus*.

The Addition of William Durand of Mende

At Rome, from the twelfth century onwards the imposition of the hand took place for each individual. The Bishop of Mende substituted this for the collective imposition of two hands in his pontifical. He also replaced the traditional

[5] See *Small Ritual* (London: Burns & Oates, 1964), p. 66.

and significant kiss of peace by an act of breathing which
he could not justify except by a dubious symbolism.

The Development of the Discipline of the Sacrament of Confirmation in the West

The increase in the number of baptisms, the spread of
places of worship, and then the preponderance of infant baptisms prevented the bishop from presiding himself at the
initiation of all the faithful according to the ancient rule.
In the East the administration of baptism and confirmation
followed one another at the same assembly, regardless of the
age of the candidate. The priest received authorisation to
give confirmation. This custom existed from the end of the
fourth century, according to the *Apostolic Constitutions*. The
authority over the sacrament, however, remained with the
bishop, since he alone, as patriarch, could consecrate the
mýron which was used for the anointing.

It was completely different in the Latin Church. From the
beginning, the rite of confirmation was reserved to bishops.
This is the teaching of Innocent I in his reply to *Decentius*
of Gubbio:

> With regard to the "signing" of babies, it is clear that only
> the bishop can do this. Ordinary priests, as they are of the
> second grade of the priesthood, have not the highest order
> which is that of the bishop. That the power of "signing" or of
> giving the Paraclete is the power of bishops alone can be seen
> not only from the practice of the Church but also from the
> passage of the Acts where it is said that Peter and John were
> sent to give the Holy Spirit to those who had been baptised.[6]

The Council of Seville in 618 was also clear about this: "It
is not allowed for priests to give the Holy Spirit to the baptised by the imposition of hands."

At Rome itself, this rule did not cause any difficulty. Confirmation was given immediately after baptism within the
framework of the rituals of Easter and Pentecost. At the
Lateran basilica the Pope himself conferred the sacrament.

---

[6] Quoted by R. Béraudy, "L'initiation chrétienne," in A. G. Martimort, ed., *L'église en prière* (Tournai: Desclée, 1965), p. 574.

In the other churches the bishops were present for this.

But outside Rome, in the rural dioceses, the bishop could not be present in all the parishes at the same time. In order to keep the sacrament of confirmation for him alone, the administration of the sacrament was separated from that of baptism. Sometimes the baptised were invited to come to the episcopal town during the octave of Easter to receive confirmation from the bishop; more often, confirmation was delayed until the next visit of the bishop to the parish, and this custom was already practiced in the sixth century in the diocese of Arles, in France.

It was in this way that confirmation was progressively delayed. In Rome, it was customary, from the seventh up to the ninth century, to confirm the neophytes, almost exclusively children, immediately after baptism. Certain dioceses in Spain and Latin America have kept this custom to the present day. Everywhere else, after the Fourth Lateran Council (1215), the custom developed of waiting for the fourth or seventh year to confirm children.

In the eighteenth and nineteenth centuries the tendency to put off the date of confirmation spread, and in certain countries (France, Belgium, Austria, Hungary) it was held back until the age of twelve years. However, in its official documents the Church did not approve this movement. The catechism of the Council of Trent fixed the age of confirmation at the age of reason; modern legislation speaks of seven years.

In certain very precise and limited cases, certain priests could receive the right to administer confirmation: but they were always extraordinary ministers of the sacrament. The bishop alone remained the ordinary minister and in all these cases he was the only minister of the consecration of the sacred chrism.

THE ESSENTIAL RITE OF CONFIRMATION

The essential rites for the administration of confirmation have undergone changes throughout the centuries, and it is very difficult to identify the absolutely essential rites at a given time.

In other parts of the Church, except Rome in the early centuries, only the imposing of hands belonged to the ritual of confirmation. The post-baptismal anointings referred only to baptism.

As we have seen, at Rome one post-baptismal anointing referred to confirmation. According to St Gregory the Great, the only essential rite of confirmation was the imposition of hands. St Jerome also relates the imposition of hands to the coming of the Holy Spirit. The *Gelasian Sacramentary* refers to this: "In order to sign them he imposes his hands with these words." But this imposition took place collectively. Therefore, in order to show the application of the effect to the individual brought about by the imposition of hands, a further rite of making the sign of the cross on each person was introduced. By the eighth century, according to Pope Gregory II, "it is necessary that the faithful be confirmed by the imposition of the hand and anointing with sacred chrism."

The liturgical books put the emphasis on the signing with chrism—i.e., the anointing—in such a way that this rite now seems the only essential one. Of course, the signing can be looked on also as imposition of the hand insofar as contact is made by the very act of making the sign of the cross.

The *Ordo Romanus Antiquus* mentions the anointing and signing and gives the formula that goes with it: "I confirm you in the name of the Father. . . ."

The Roman Pontifical of the twelfth century already had the formula used nowadays. "I sign you with the sign of the Cross, I confirm you with the chrism of salvation, in the name of the Father. . . ."

The documents of the teaching authority are content at first to base one rite on the other, seeing an imposition of hands in the anointing with chrism.

In 1274, for example, in the profession of faith of Michael Paleologus, the words occur: "The Sacrament of Confirmation which is given by the bishop through the imposition of hands as he anoints those who are baptised."

The great scholastic writers, however, have no hesitation

about dropping the reference to the imposition of hands: they define the matter of the sacrament as the anointing with chrism, and the form as the formula pronounced when the anointing is given. This teaching was rendered official by subsequent official documents which, up to and including the Council of Trent, do not refer any longer to the imposition of hands.

In the eighteenth century Benedict XIV wanted to restore continuity with the old custom. Changing the rubrics of the Pontifical, he prescribed that the minister should put his hands flat on the head of the person to be confirmed during the anointing, and such is the custom which is in force nowadays, since the code of 1917 and the new Roman Ritual. The imposition of hands and the unction with oil are Biblical signs: it is in the light of their Biblical symbolism that we can understand the grace of consecration which they produce.

So, as I have said, from the standpoint of its ritual, confirmation has not always been the same. The original essential rite in the Roman liturgy was the general imposition of hands with the invocation of the Holy Spirit. This still remains, but it is now an accessory rite. According to replies given by the Holy See, the sacrament is not repeated, even conditionally, if this rite has been omitted. An anointing was introduced into the confirmation ritual at a very early date. It is now the essential rite in the West as well as in the East.[7]

THE PRESENT RITE OF CONFIRMATION

The ceremony is opened with the hymn *Veni Creator Spiritus,* followed by a talk from the bishop. The bishop then stands facing the candidates and recites the *Omnipotens,* the first short prayer asking for the Holy Spirit to come down upon those to be confirmed. (The "coming down" of the Holy Spirit must not be taken too literally. The Holy Spirit does not come by moving from one place to another, from an imaginary heaven to a space within us. The Spirit comes by establishing or strengthening a relation with us, and all the

[7] Davis, *op. cit.,* p. 140.

change this involves takes place on our side.[8]) The *Omni-potens* opens by recalling the two aspects of baptismal grace. This prayer, in its essentials, goes back to the second century, but the present form dates from the seventh or eighth century.

After this mention of the divine goodness at the moment of baptism, the Church asks God to send down from heaven the sevenfold Holy Spirit, the Paraclete, on those to be confirmed. The enumeration of the seven gifts of the Spirit is a reference to the text of the Vulgate (Isaiah 11:2). The prayer stresses the configuration between those to be confirmed and the Messiah King announced by the prophet, for Isaiah referred these gifts to the Messiah King. The prayer ends by relating the spiritual signing of Christians to the material signing of which they are to be the object: "Sign them with the sign of the Cross of Christ."

This prayer is followed by several verses and responses. The bishop then stretches out his hands over the candidates, showing by this dramatic gesture that he is going to transmit to them the Holy Spirit. At the same time he utters the ancient solemn invocation of the Spirit and his gifts already referred to.

The candidates now go up in turn for the anointing with chrism. The bishop, puts it on their foreheads as he makes sign of the cross, speaking the words of the formula of administration already mentioned. The laying on of hands by the bishop is a symbol of the power and authority given by this sacrament of initiation to Christians to witness to Christ. The consecration with chrism, which is olive oil mixed with sweet-smelling balsam, is a sign that they are made like to Christ, who was anointed for his work of Messiah. Its sweet, very pervasive smell shows the candidate that he must be ready to spread the knowledge of God everywhere like the perfume. The tracing of the sign of the cross on the forehead of the candidates is a sign that they must be ready to confess their faith openly and without shame. The cross represents suffering: they must be prepared to suffer for Christ with the strength given by the Holy Spirit. The cross is also the

[8] *Ibid.*, p. 167.

sign of victory which Christ gained through his crucifixion, and this is a reminder to the candidates that through the suffering and the merits of Christ they will attain the victory of the eternal life.

The bishop strikes each candidate lightly on the cheek when he has anointed him. This is meant as a gesture of affection, as indeed it is in everyday usage, even nowadays. It is actually a substitute for the ancient kiss of peace, and is intended to show the love and affection of the bishop as he welcomes the confirmed Christians as new witnesses to Christ, and as assistants to himself in spreading the faith.

In the thirteenth century, the fact that confirmation is the sacrament of strength made William Durand interpret this gesture as a blow, symbolising the sufferings that Christians must endure as they fulfil the duty of witnessing to Christ which the sacrament has imposed on them.

The antiphon, which is one of frequent use in the liturgy, has a special meaning with regard to confirmation because of its reference to strength and because the words come from one of the great Pentecostal psalms (Psalm 68), the Roman liturgy (as Fr O'Shea notes[9]): "Confirm O God what thou has wrought in us from thy holy temple in Jerusalem." The application is clear: God will make the grace of confirmation effective and the Spirit who has come down from heaven on the confirmed will complete the work he has begun.

After the individual anointings, there are prayers for the confirmed including *Deus, qui apostolis tuis,* which goes back to the tenth century. This closing prayer contains a two-fold instruction. It says that the Holy Spirit who has just been given is the "Spirit of Pentecost." His coming is to prepare those who have been confirmed to be active workers in the building of the kingdom of God. The full prayer is:

> O God who didst give thy Holy Spirit to the Apostles and didst will that through them and through those who should come after them, he should be given to the rest of the faithful; look favourably upon this humble fulfilment of our office, and grant that the same Holy Spirit, coming into the heart of

[9] O'Shea, *op. cit.,* p. 60. But note the version given in the Jerusalem Bible (v. 28–29) is slightly different from that of the Ritual and the point is rather lost.

(him) whose forehead we have marked with Sacred Chrism and signed with the sign of the Holy Cross, may dwell therein and make of it a living temple of his glory. Who lives and reigns for ever. Amen.

Just as the Holy Spirit dwelt in the soul of Jesus and made it holy, and as he came down upon the apostles to make them prophets and witnesses, so now he comes to each Christian to continue in him the work of the Incarnation and the Redemption. The wonder of Pentecost is renewed, without the striking outward manifestations that marked that event, but no less really and completely.

A blessing concludes the whole rite:

"Thus shall every man be blessed who fears the Lord. . . . May the Lord bless you from Sion, and all the days of your earthly life keep before your eyes the treasures of the heavenly Jerusalem. And may eternal life be yours. Amen.[10]

The blessings of the new covenant—sonship, joy, life, intimacy with God—are the "good things of Jerusalem" which God bestows through the working of the Holy Spirit in us. We enjoy them in this life, but they are ordered and directed toward the final object of the divine plan: eternal life in the Jerusalem that is above. They secure that life for us in advance and bring us safely to the eternal possession of it.[11]

THE GODPARENTS OF CONFIRMATION

The Code of Canon Law and the ritual prescribe godparents for confirmation. In principle, it is not permissible for only one godparent to present all the candidates, as was formerly done very frequently. The godparent, who must be of the same sex as the godchild, should only present one person for confirmation, or two at the most. The application of these principles in recent years has been the cause of a very fruitful pastoral effort to associate the whole community with the formation of those who are to be confirmed and to put

[10] *Small Ritual,* p. 67.
[11] O'Shea, *op. cit.,* p. 61.

them into contact with adults who are deeply engaged in the apostolate of the Church.

The modern law has not suppressed the old law against the godparent of baptism being the same as the godparent of confirmation, unless these two sacraments are conferred at the same time in one and the same ceremony. This surprising rule is modified by the faculty which is given to the minister to dispense with it for any reasonable cause. It comes, in any case, from a false interpretation of the text of the ancient law.

THE MINISTER OF CONFIRMATION

The ordinary minister of confirmation in the West is the bishop.

In the East, priests were allowed, as we have seen, to give confirmation, and still are. This custom goes back to the fourth century, but the bishop's jurisdiction over the sacrament and the idea that the priests confirm as delegates of the bishop are shown by the fact that he alone consecrates the mýron or chrism.

In 1946, Pope Pius XII gave parish priests the power to confirm their subjects in danger of death. The Church has the power, within limits, to designate the minister of the sacrament, the power of which comes from Christ, who is able to use either as a minister. There is room for a further extension of this faculty, if episcopal conferences, especially in mission countries, think fit.

THE TIME OF RECEPTION
OF CONFIRMATION

Originally, as we have seen, the sacraments of initiation were given together to adults and infants in this order: baptism, confirmation, Holy Eucharist. Thus the unity of Christian initiation was clearly shown.

Circumstances forced separation of the rites in the West. Still, up to the twelfth century the three sacraments were given together when there was a bishop to administer them.

Even infants were given the three sacraments in one ceremony.

When confirmation was delayed, the order mentioned above was still kept.

In the Western Church, the practice spread of not giving communion to infants or children before the "age of discretion." Since the tenth century, children had been given communion in the form of a few drops of the consecrated wine. This practice was dropped about the beginning of the thirteenth century when the faithful ceased to communicate in both kinds. The Fourth Lateran Council in 1215, by laying down the obligation of an annual Easter communion only for those who had reached the age of discretion, implicitly approved the practice of delaying communion until that age. It was already the general custom by then and has remained so ever since. However, there have been various interpretations of the age of discretion. At various times and places we find the age of discretion placed somewhere between seven and twelve, or even frequently at fourteen or fifteen. Shortly after the Lateran Council the custom began, as we have seen, of deferring confirmation. The practice was not uniform—it was deferred variously until the age of one, or three, or even twelve. Nevertheless, it was always given before communion (the Anglican Church in England still keeps this practice).

The Catechism of the Council of Trent issued in 1566 had the effect of firmly establishing the practice of not giving confirmation before the age of seven (referred to as the "age of reason"). The Council of Trent puts it this way: "Here it is to be observed that after baptism the sacrament of confirmation may indeed be administered to all; but until children have attained the use of reason, its administration is not expedient. If it does not seem well to defer confirmation until the age of twelve, it is most proper to postpone this sacrament at least till after seven years." Not before seven years but not later than twelve years—this became the general practice in the West except in some dioceses in Spain and Latin America where the custom of confirming infants together with baptism is still retained.

All the same, for centuries it remained the practice everywhere to give confirmation before communion. It was not until the nineteenth century that the custom grew up of leaving confirmation until after first communion. When Pope Pius X, in 1910, brought the age of first communion back again to seven, this had the effect of perpetuating the reversal of order between confirmation and communion. The Code of Canon Law in 1917 said that the sacrament of confirmation in the Latin Church is fittingly deferred until about the seventh years of age but it may be given earlier in danger of death or any just and serious reason. In 1931, this law was interpreted to mean that confirmation must not be given in the Latin Church before about the seventh year except in the circumstances mentioned. The Sacred Congregation of Sacraments in 1932 said that it is opportune and more in conformity with the nature and effects of the sacrament of confirmation that children should not come to the holy table for the first time until they have received confirmation, which is like the complement of baptism and in which the Holy Spirit is given. The Decision continues, however, stressing that, on the other hand, children should not be forbidden access to the holy table if they have come to the age of reason, without having been previously to receive the sacrament of confirmation.

THE EFFECTS OF CONFIRMATION

The difficulty in distinguishing the special effects of confirmation arises from the fact that the sacraments of initiation were so bound up together that it was difficult to differentiate them.

Nevertheless, it is possible to affirm that, from the third century onwards, confirmation was regarded as completing and perfecting baptism by a *special* gift of the Holy Spirit. It is important to stress that it is a *special* gift of the Spirit because the Holy Spirit is really given in baptism. There can be no sanctification, no birth to supernatural life without this gift. ("Unless a man is born through water and the Spirit. . . .")

What do we mean when we say that confirmation completes or "perfects" baptism? First of all, we do *not* mean that there is something imperfect about baptism and that confirmation remedies that imperfection. Rather we mean that confirmation adds a new spiritual dimension to the being or status of the baptised person. Baptism is often compared to a child—by nature a human being but not a "perfect" human being in the same sense that a full grown man is. Applying this child-adult comparison to the supernatural realities of baptism and confirmation sheds a certain amount of light, but the comparison is rather derogatory to baptism if taken too far. Sometimes the primary and distinctive effect of confirmation has been obscured by the failure to stress the special nature of the gift of the Holy Spirit as given in confirmation. It has been widely said that confirmation gives greater grace and a fuller measure of the Holy Spirit: but so does every sacrament.

The natural and best way to bring out the primary and distinctive effect of confirmation is by analogy with Our Lord himself.

In the life of Christ, there were two anointings by the Spirit. The first was at the moment of the Incarnation: this anointing established him as the Son of God. This is the hypostatic union, in which Jesus was constituted king and priest at the same time; it was a *royal* and *priestly* consecration affecting the being of Jesus.

The other anointing took place when he was baptised in the Jordan. At that moment he accepted his mission as the "servant of God" prophesied in the Old Testament, the Messiah-Redeemer. He was anointed as the one destined to play the chief role in God's plan of redemption and salvation for mankind.

These two separate anointings are reproduced in the life of a Christian: the divine adopted sonship is given by baptism. The role of sharing in Christ's redemptive work is conferred by confirmation.

In other words, baptism sanctifies the Christian as an individual; confirmation gives him an official social outgoing role in the Church and to the world.

To see confirmation's primary effect on the individual Christian, we must consider the gift of the Spirit to the Church and its first members at Pentecost. Just as Pentecost is a distinct and necessary event within the Paschal mystery, so confirmation has a unique function in the life of the Christian which is not performed or substituted for by any of the other sacraments. Before the apostles could preach to the world, spread the faith, found the Church, they had to receive the separate special gift of the Spirit: only with the gift of the Spirit at Pentecost did they—the Church—become the mystical body of Christ filled with and led by his Spirit. Only then could she act in continuing Christ's work on earth, as the mystical extension of his bodily presence on earth to bring the good news of salvation to all, as his mystical body. The risen Christ gave his Spirit at Pentecost so that through the members of his Church he could go out and transform the world.

In confirmation, then, the gift of the Spirit comes to the Christian so as to overflow from him *to others:* the Christian becomes the source of the Spirit for others.

Baptism initiates man into the community of the disciples of Christ, the new people of God. Being baptised, each member has a share in Christ's mission because the Church is essentially missionary. But the mission given at baptism is given to the *individual* member of the Church: it requires confirming or perfecting so that individual activity may become part of the action of the Church as a whole. Confirmation gives a "character" or added official status in the Church, enabling the recipient to act in this new social dimension. A confirmed Christian is a more responsible apostle, for he has been given this discipleship officially and permanently by the community which is the Church. A confirmed Christian has a closer relationship to Christ in his kingly, priestly, and prophetic role. It is for this reason that confirmation is the sacrament most intimately connected with the laity. With baptism it is the foundation of the dignity of the faithful.

The renewal and upgrading of the role of the laity after Vatican II is not a purely or primarily sociological phenomenon, showing that the laity want "more say" in the Church, that the Church should be more democratically organised and give a greater share of its life as a society to the vast majority of its members who are not priests. These sociological factors have their influence and validity, but the fundamental reason why the laity should not merely be required "to pay, pray and obey" as in the past, stems from the great spiritual dignity conferred on them by baptism and confirmation.

This, then, is the first main effect of confirmation—the gift of the Holy Spirit in order that the one confirmed may fulfil an apostolic, missionary role as witness. For this the properties of the Holy Spirit are required and given.

A digression may usefully be made here. In the past the emphasis has often been on the strengthening effect of confirmation, suggested by the very name (which means "to strengthen" and can also mean "to establish"). The name and the idea come from the words of an early homily, attributed to Pope Melchiades, referring to "strength for battle." The sacrament was regarded as strengthening the Christian for battle, making him a soldier of Jesus Christ. This meaning, although rather narrow, can be accepted, especially if it is understood in the way the Council of Florence (1439) described it:

> The effect of the sacrament consists in this, that the Holy Spirit is given for the strengthening of the Christian, just as he was given to the apostles on the day of Pentecost, the purpose being that the Christian may boldly "profess the name of Christ."

The Christian is anointed in confirmation to be a martyr, which, in its original meaning, meant a witness. It came to be applied to those who suffered for their faith, for they were witnesses *par excellence* to the faith. But it applies, as does the word "prophet," to any courageous witnessing and proclaiming of the Gospel—which is the role to which each confirmed person is committed by his very confirmation.

This witnessing does not mean preaching in the ordinary sense of the word. It can manifest itself in the kind of people we are and the kind of life we lead. The early Christians gave this witness by the way they showed love, prompting people to observe, "See how these Christians love each other."

A twentieth-century businessman could "witness" by being a man of integrity, scrupulously honest in his dealings, and concerned for social justice.

In other words, the witness we give means professing our faith, in our particular circumstances of life, whatever the cost.

This may well involve explaining the faith to others when the opportunity arises; for those who are able it may well find expression in joining one of the many organisations which provide opportunity for exercise of the lay apostolate.

But it is important to recognise that one of the most important ways of professing the faith is to take part in the public worship of the Church. The Holy Spirit inspires many activities of different kinds, many of which may be concerned with the material welfare of our fellow man, but such a witness divorced from the public worship of the Church, or making little of it, is not a true Christian witness. Christian witness does not merely mean engaging in philanthropic or secular activities for their own sake, without reference to the Holy Spirit who moves us.

This does not mean that Christians must give a specifically religious character to their social work, for example, or insist on giving associations which work for "good causes" a specifically Christian or Catholic character. Indeed, their witness in secular fields will often consist in working in an ecumenical spirit with members of other churches, of other religions, or of none. But the Catholic Christian, in the spirit of *Gaudium et Spes,* while he works for the perfecting of this world, will not regard this as the only thing in life. He will realise also that this is not an abiding city and that the two commands—to love and worship God and to love and save his neighbour—are complementary. "We must do the one and not omit the other." For example, for a Catholic to campaign for civil rights with others is very laudable and necessary: to regard that as fully satisfying his *religious* duties so that he need not bother with the worship of God would be to take too short a view of Christian life. On the other hand, to regard racial injustice as no concern of his because he was intent on the worship of God would be equally wrong.

One of the faults in the child-adult analogy used to illustrate the different effects of baptism and confirmation is that it takes a child several years to grow to physical maturity, but in the order of grace the full maturity, the full development of our Christian life, takes but a few moments by the power of God. A small child given confirmation receives the completion of his divine sonship and the "anointing" for his role in the Church—all in a few moments. This effect needs to be developed, but nevertheless it is there. This is not a question of physical or physiological or psychological or moral or ascetical maturity. It is a maturity of Christian being. Thus, when we speak of "perfect" Christians, we must forget altogether the meaning of "perfect" in the moral and especially the ascetical sense. No Christian is perfect in that sense. But confirmation gives the Christian his full Christian stature. A grown man is a man even though he may have many physical or psychological imperfections, and a confirmed Christian is a "perfect" Christian even though he may have many sins and imperfections and be far from perfect in the ordinary meaning of the word.

As Father O'Shea says:

> The seven gifts of the Spirit effect a smoother functioning of the life of Christ in us. They render us more prompt to respond to the urgings of the Spirit, the demands that the Christ life makes upon us. Insofar as we can say such a thing, they make it easier for us to live the supernatural life; they make it, as it were, natural. Under the influence of the gifts we find it relatively easy to withstand temptation, to pray, to worship, to follow the right course of action. It is true that this pre-supposes co-operation and the right dispositions on our part, but the gifts are there for the using. Again the difference between the saints and most of us is that they make use of the gifts to the full whilst so many of us let them remain idle.[12]

As confirmation is the completion of baptism, it must perfect the main effects of baptism which are two: the conferring of the divine sonship and the consecration to God's service in worship (by the character). Confirmation, then, is the maturing and the deepening of our consecration to God and

[12] O'Shea, op. cit., p. 65.

of our sonship of the heavenly Father. It is thus a deepening, too, of our configuration to Christ as priest. We became members of a priestly people, deputed to the worship of God. Confirmation, by configuring us to Christ the prophet, completes the likeness to Christ the priest, because these two functions are closely connected.

THE PRIESTHOOD OF THE LAITY

A special effect of confirmation is to complete the status of confirmed persons as part of the royal priesthood, in which, as St Peter says, all Christians participate. It may be useful here to pause and consider what this priesthood means.

St Leo the Great (who died in 461) has a beautiful passage on the occasion of the celebration of the anniversary of his consecration as a bishop:

> You have good reason to celebrate this anniversary; for by baptism, according to the teaching of St Peter, the royal dignity of the priesthood is common to you all. The anointing of the Holy Spirit has consecrated all of you as priests. It is good and religious that you should rejoice in our elevation as an honour in which you yourselves share. And even if the mysterious grace of him who holds it descends with great abundance upon members who hold high place, it flows with no sparing generosity upon those of lower degree.[13]

This royal priesthood means that the laity really take part in the liturgy—sharing in Christ's priesthood. It is baptism and confirmation which give them the right and status to do so.

The text of the Liturgy Constitution gives witness to this priestly character of participation in the liturgy.

> Rightly, then, the liturgy is considered as an exercise of the priestly office of Jesus Christ. In the Liturgy the sanctification of man is manifested by signs perceptible to the senses, and is effected in a way which is proper to each of these signs; in the Liturgy full public worship is performed by the mystical body of Jesus Christ, that is, by the Head and His members. From this it follows that every liturgical celebration, because it is an action of Christ the priest and of His body the Church, is a

[13] Sermo #4, *Patrologia Latina*, 54, 148.

sacred action surpassing all others. No other action of the Church can match its efficacy, match its claim to nor equal the degree of it. (No. 7)[14]

The greater active participation in the liturgy to which the Council has given great impetus is not just a move to give a greater importance to the laity as modern circumstances might seem to warrant. It is a natural consequence of the priestly role they are called on to play. The Constitution on the Church is worth quoting in full on this point.

Christ the Lord, High Priest taken from among men (Cf. Heb. 5:1–5) made a Kingdom and priests to God his Father (Apoc. 1:6; cf. 5:9–10) out of this new people. The baptised, by regeneration and the anointing of the Holy Spirit, are consecrated into a spiritual house and a holy priesthood. Thus through all those works befitting Christian men they can offer spiritual sacrifices and proclaim the power of Him who has called them out of darkness into His marvellous light (cf. 1 Pet. 2:4–10). Therefore all the disciples of Christ, persevering in prayer and praising God (cf. Acts 2:42–47), should present themselves as living sacrifice, holy and pleasing to God (cf. Rom. 12:1). Everywhere on earth they must bear witness to Christ and give an answer to those who seek an account of that hope of eternal life which is in them (cf. 1 Pet. 3:15).

Though they differ from one another in essence and not only in degree, the common priesthood of the faithful and the ministerial or hierarchical priesthood are nonetheless inter-related. Each of them in its own special way is a participation in the one priesthood of Christ. The ministerial priest, by the sacred power he enjoys, molds and rules the priestly people. Acting in the person of Christ, he brings about the Eucharistic Sacrifice, and offers it to God in the name of all the people. For their part, the faithful join in the offering of the Eucharist by virtue of their royal priesthood. They likewise exercise that priesthood by receiving the sacraments, by prayer and thanks-giving, by the witness of a holy life, and by self-denial and active charity.

It is through the sacraments and the exercise of the virtues that the sacred nature and organic structure of the priestly community is brought into operation. Incorporated into the Church through baptism, the faithful are consecrated by the baptismal character to the exercise of the cult of the Christian

[14] Walter M. Abbot, S.J., ed., *The Documents of Vatican II* (New York: American Press, 1966), p. 141.

religion. Reborn as sons of God, they must confess before men the faith which they have received from God through the Church. Bound more intimately to the Church by the sacrament of confirmation, they are endowed by the Holy Spirit with special strength. Hence they are more strictly obliged to spread and defend the faith both by word and by deed as true witnesses of Christ.

Taking part in the Eucharistic Sacrifice which is the fount and apex of the whole Christian life, they offer the divine Victim to God, and offer themselves along with It . . . (Nos. 10,11).[15]

The last paragraph deals particularly with the priestly office. The common priesthood of all the baptised provides the basis for, and requires for its completion, the ministerial priesthood of the ordained clergy[16] (Note 30).

The faithful act as priest, then, particularly in the Eucharistic sacrifice but also by the consecration of their lives to the glory of God with all their activities, corporal as well as spiritual, social as well as individual.

A priest's work is to consecrate and make sacred by virtue of his office: the faithful laity do this by virtue of the office given them in baptism and confirmation.

But this priesthood of the laity upgrades the role of the faithful without downgrading the role of the ordained priest and consecrated bishop. The sacrament of holy orders gives a further character which makes the difference between the faithful and the ordained priest one of essence.

The priest receives a special anointing to give him a special share in the priesthood of Christ: this gives the power of consecrating the Eucharistic sacrifice and exercising hierarchic authority in the Church (in the case of bishops, in fullness of power; in the case of priests, as assistants and deputies of the bishop). The authority conferred by sacred orders gives the priest the office of ministering to and guiding the faithful. This authority is not one of domination but of service. Nevertheless, it is very real. It has been given by Christ for the sanctification of the whole people of God so

[15] *Ibid.*, pp. 26–28.
[16] *Ibid.*, p. 27, n. 30.

that they will transform the world for Christ. In the action of the sacraments we see this sanctifying function—and especially in the Eucharistic sacrifice, where it is most apparent that the consecrating function of the priest enables the people of God to exercise that priesthood.

From this it follows that there is not, and should not be, a gulf between clergy and laity or an antagonism between them. The one mission of Christ is the work of the Holy Spirit carried on in the Church. Pastors and the faithful share in this mission of Christ to the world. All are apostles: they are complementary. In the past the great potential and even the role of the laity have been neglected. What is now required is not less respect for priests in their sacred character, but more respect for the laity based on the character acquired in baptism and confirmation. But there are no second-class citizens in the kingdom of God. If the work of the Church is the mission of Christ, it is to be done by one harmonious team of disciples. Anticlericalism—insofar as it wishes to get rid of acquired customs which have obscured the pastoral role of the hierarchy, or the ministry of service which they exercise—can be a *good* thing. Anticlericalism which seeks to minimise the sacred role of the priests or their special ministry to the people of God for which they have been ordained is a *bad* thing, especially when it arises out of jealousy, out of discontent or out of a desire to blur the distinction between faithful and priests or to undermine their rightful authority.

The basic duty of priests and laity is to imitate the love of Christ for his Church and for each other, so that there should be one people of God, not rent by divisions, but united in prolonging the mission of Christ himself upon earth.

It is important to stress the fact that confirmation is intended to strengthen us in our missionary role of witnesses. It is not intended—as some people have thought, and as pagan societies have used rites of initiation—to help directly in the struggles of adolescence. The sacraments for this are the Eucharist and penance. While accepting this, some persons have suggested a later age for confirmation than seven, so that confirmation should be given at the end of childhood. In England and Germany there is considerable support for this[17] but as we have seen this is not of a directly theological nature and would stem rather from the idea of a full personal participation in the sacrament.

Within the context of a true understanding of the sacrament, pastoral reasons may suggest a later age for its more effectual administration. The main argument in favour of a late age, it seems to me, is the desirability of a full personal participation in this sacrament which is given only once. The necessity of baptism for salvation precludes a personal participation in their baptism for those born of Christian parents; they are baptised as infants. Is there not some advantage, particularly in the circumstances of a post-Christian society, in having a full, active, personal sharing in the second stage of initiation, confirmation. Presumably this is the reason for delaying confirmation until seven, the age of reason. But is not seven too early to secure an active, personal commitment to Christ in the full meaning of the phrase? We are told that to delay confirmation is to upset the traditional order of the sacraments of initiation and take away part of the meaning of confirmation, by making it follow first communion. But here facts must be faced, and we must talk about the real situation. Unless first communion is wrongly deferred, it is inevitable that most children will receive confirmation *after* their first communion.[18]

The Vatican Council (Liturgy Constitution) does not decide this question. It merely states: "The rite of confirmation is to be revised and the intimate connection which this sacrament has with the whole process of Christian initiation is to be more lucidly set forth" (No. 71).[19]

THE GIFTS OF THE HOLY SPIRIT

The gifts of the Holy Spirit are enumerated in Isaiah 11:2–4: "One shall be born, on whom the spirit of the Lord will rest, a spirit wise and discerning, a spirit prudent and

[17] Archbishop Beck of Liverpool, for example, and Cardinal Urbani of Venice have recently said (September, 1966): "Confirmation should be deferred to the end of compulsory education." *The Tablet,* 17th September, 1966, p. 1056.
[18] C. Davis, p. 160.
[19] *The Documents of Vatican II,* p. 160.

strong, a spirit of knowledge and of piety, and ever fear of the Lord shall fill his heart." [20]

These are the gifts of the Holy Spirit that dwell in the Messiah and are given to us to show our configuration to Christ.

THE CHARACTER OF BAPTISM
AND CONFIRMATION

The character of confirmation completes our status in the worshipping community by giving that membership a social and apostolic dimension. The liturgy of the Church is the centre where the mission to the world is constantly renewed. The confirmed person is thus an apt subject to receive from the bishop some part in the official teaching work of the Church—as teachers of religious doctrines in schools have done, and those devoted people who give catechetical lessons to those in non-Catholic schools by special authorisation of the bishop.

The English catechism says that a character is a mark or seal upon the soul which cannot be effaced, and therefore the sacrament conferring it may not be repeated. A good deal of explanation is necessary for this definition. It is useful at once to distinguish the two distinct, but connected, uses of the word "seal." It is also more convenient to deal with the character of baptism and of confirmation together, since they are so closely connected. "Seal" in the early Church, indeed in the New Testament, is a common word used to mean "baptism."

A few words about that meaning of "seal" will therefore be useful before we proceed to speak about the character or special seal of the sacraments of initiation.

As early as the middle of the second century, the term "seal" was used as a synonym for "baptism," baptism being considered the complex of initiation rites. *The Shepherd of*

---

[20] I have used the Knox version of Isaiah because this, following the Vulgate and Septuagate, gives the *seven* gifts. In the Jerusalem Bible only six are given because piety and fear of the Lord are combined.

Hermas, written between 140 and 155 and read in the churches, was quoted by Irenaeus of Gaul, by Tertullian in Africa, by Clement of Alexandria, and by Origen. It speaks of a person's "receiving the seal," where we should say the person "has been baptised": "Before a man has borne the name of the Son of God he is dead; but when he has received the seal, he layeth aside his deadness and resumeth life. The seal, then, is the water; they go down into the water dead and they come up alive." [21] Clement of Alexandria tells the story of the young man whom St John converted and entrusted to the care of a presbyter, who was most vigilant until "after having enlightened him," i.e. baptised him, he lessened his former care and guard of the young man, having given him the perfect guard, the seal of the Lord.

St Basil, speaking of Philip's dealing with the Ethiopian servant returning to the Queen of Ethiopia, remarks that he did not delay the seal. When they came to water, he said, "Here is water, what prevents me from being baptised?" [22]

The texts of the New Testament and of the Fathers give a clear foundation for the doctrine that the sealing of the Christian in baptism impresses an enduring mark on the soul. The Fathers use these texts and others in sacred scripture in their assertion that by baptism the Christian is marked and sealed by God as his own. They speak of the seal in instructions about baptism in order to enhance the dignity of the Christian state, to comfort and give assurance that the seal is a protection against temptation and the powers of evil, and to exhort to a worthy Christian life.

The Fathers use many comparisons in discussing the seal. It is compared to the brand burnt upon animals to denote ownership. Very frequently it is also compared to the military branding or tattooing, a mark which soldiers bore as a sign of service, a means of recognition, and a precaution against desertion. St Ambrose speaks of the "character" of Christ

[21] Bernard Leeming, S.J., *Principles of Sacramental Theology* (2d. ed.; London: Longmans, 1966), p. 162.

[22] I am indebted to Brother Leeming, *op. cit.,* for his comprehensive treatment of the "seal," pp. 162 ff.

which Valentinian bore within him just as slaves are marked with the character or ownership mark of their masters, or soldiers with the name of the emperor. The seal was like the military mark which implied a life engagement in the army of Christ. The seal is also compared to the device on a ring which stamps a document as a guarantee of authenticity. St Gregory of Nazianzen makes the interesting comment that the personal work of the minister does not affect the sacrament, since the seal, whether made of iron or of gold, impresses itself equally upon the wax. Tertullian speaks of the seal of contract on a document. Sometimes the seal is compared to the inscription of an image on a coin. St Irenaeus said that we receive through the Spirit the image and superscription of the Father and the Son. St Paul compared baptism to circumcision, and St Cyril of Jerusalem, commenting on this, says: "By likeness in faith we come to the sonship of Abraham and then our faith, like his, receives a spiritual seal being circumcised by the Holy Ghost through the sacred washing in circumcision, not of the body but of the heart. . . ." Baptism is also compared to the marking of the door post of the Israelites with the blood of the Paschal lamb; the seal marks the souls of the faithful so that the angel of vengeance passes by.

There is also comparison with the sealing up of something to secure its safety, as we seal a registered letter or a money bag. St Basil warns, for example, "Unsealed treasure is easily laid hold on by thieves."

These comparisons show that the doctrine of the seal was generally accepted. The Fathers taught that baptism would give remission of sins, illumination, the adoption of sonship, the indwelling of the Holy Spirit, and membership in the Body of Christ; but they also taught that baptism gives the seal, the imprint of God, upon the soul.

To sum up, then, the doctrine of the Church before the time of St Augustine, all comparisons used by Christian writers tend to emphasise the indelible nature of the seal, and fit perfectly into the general conviction that baptism once received can never be repeated. Grace admittedly could be lost. Several Fathers of the second and third centuries say that the seal may be stained, defaced, or damaged, but never suggest that it may be lost or totally destroyed. Origen specifically says that the seal is conferred upon those who receive baptism in sin, though to their condemnation. In the fourth century, the seal is called "unbreakable and indelible" and it is noteworthy that St John Chrysostom says it is a mark which manifests "discerners," and St Basil said that in sinners it carries with it a certain presence of the Holy Ghost who looks for their conversion.

Consequently, when St Augustine, about the year 390, maintained that baptism imprints an indelible mark upon the soul, and that this mark is distinct from grace, he had ample warrant in the earlier tradition of the Church.[23]

Before the time of St Augustine—that is, up to the year 380 or thereabouts—there had been two broad currents of thought in the Church which seemed to flow in different channels: the one, concerned with the "seal" impressed upon the soul in Christian initiation; the other, with the refusal to repeat sacraments of initiation. It was Augustine who first clearly perceived that these two streams really converged. The doctrine of the "seal" meant that grace was not the sole gift at the time one becomes a Christian; the "seal" was another gift, different from grace, and this gift explained why baptism was not repeated.

When Augustine spoke of the character, he voiced two heartfelt convictions. The first was that God's Holy Spirit does not limit his activity merely to the good and the orthodox, but extends it even to the wicked and the heretical. The second was that all Christians ought to revere the consecration given in Christian baptism. Belief in the character means that the Christian becomes holy not only by voluntary union with God but also by a lasting dedication caused by God's action upon his soul. By baptism the Christian becomes a person permanently dedicated, christened after the pattern of Christ. As Christ's union with God was not merely a moral or "ethical" union, made by harmony of mind and will, as the Nestorians held, but was a union of the very being of Christ with God, so likewise the Christian is united to

[23] Leeming, op. cit., p. 178.

God not only by mind and will but by a certain quality given to his being. There is a real basis for the new juridical state which the baptised person acquires, and acquires for ever; and this is reflected in the new relationships to God and to human society which that state carries. The finality of God's revelation and redemption in Christ is imaged in the finality of Christian baptism. Once and for all, man is made a Christian, even as the Son of God was made the man Christ once and for all. As the Incarnation is God's work, so also is baptism, and so also are its irrevocable dedication and consecration. Baptism is, of course, freely accepted; but it cannot be freely repudiated. The character of Christ given to the baptised can never be lost. "It is clear," Augustine says, "that baptism does remain inseparably in the baptised person, because into whatever depth of evil, and into whatever fearful whirlpool of sin he may fall, even to the ruin of apostasy, he yet is not bereft of his baptism." [24]

Father Leeming says that during the four hundred years preceding the Council of Trent there had been in the Church an explicit belief that character was conferred by confirmation and holy orders as well as by baptism. Theologians of the twelfth century had taken its existence for granted and had discussed its functions and qualities. Great theologians of the thirteenth century, Albert the Great, Thomas Aquinas, Bonaventure Scotus, and their commentators all did likewise, and the matter entered the common law of the Church by way of Gratian's Decretums and its commentators.

One definition in the thirteenth century was "a character is a holy sign of the communion of Saints and of holy ordination, conferred hierarchically." St Thomas suggests that this might be better put as "a sign of communication of power with regard to divine things and ordination, given by the divine Blessedness." The Council of Florence in 1439 said that baptism, confirmation, and orders "imprint an indelible sign on the soul, that is, a certain character distinctive from the others. Hence they should not be repeated in the same person." [25] The Council of Trent adopted this definition,

[24] *Ibid.*, p. 132.
[25] Denziger 695.

saying that "certain spiritual and indelible marks when these sacraments are given cannot be repeated."

We have already seen that it was difficult in the early Church, especially outside Rome, to distinguish confirmation and its essential rites from baptism. By the thirteenth century, however, it was agreed that confirmation also confers an indelible character, although this may be only an enhancement or further modification or perfecting of the baptismal character, just as confirmation is the perfecting in the sense of complementing baptism.

There is solid foundation for this in the Fathers even before Augustine. The main argument is drawn from the fact that the rites of initiation, including confirmation, were never repeated. Confirmation, no matter how it was given—by imposition of hands, by a signing with the sign of the cross, or by an anointing—was not repeated. Now, as we have seen, St Augustine proceeded from the fact that baptism could not be repeated to an argument for the existence of the baptismal character. The argument holds good for confirmation. All the evidence, then, which shows that baptism and confirmation are distinct sacraments, will tend also to show that confirmation confers an indelible character. Even though confirmation is a distinct sacrament, there is no reason to doubt that it confers a character, or at least perfects and modifies the baptismal character.

It will be realised that all that has been said about confirmation, together with the teaching of the Vatican Council —which is based on new insights into baptism and confirmation—is not compatible with the idea of a Christian as an introverted individualist concerned about his own soul and his own salvation but leaving those of others to priests and professional lay apostles. Every Christian, by being a full member of the Church, is by that very fact an apostle and a missionary, commissioned to be concerned and responsible for the spreading of God's truth, of God's plan of salvation. The way he exercises this role will depend on circumstances, as we have seen. If it is true in the natural order that "no man is an island," this is even more valid in the supernatural order.

CHAPTER V

THE HOLY EUCHARIST

Some theologians, including Karl Rahner, do not include Holy Eucharist in the sacraments of Christian initiation. This is certainly justifiable from one point of view, namely that the Holy Eucharist is a sacrament which continues throughout life and is often repeated and which goes far beyond the original stage of initiation into Christian life. In this sense baptism and confirmation make a Christian fully initiated, and as fully initiated Christians they take part in the Holy Eucharist.

While this is true under this one aspect, the unity between the rites in the early initiation ceremonies, the emphasis the Fathers put on this unity, and the fact that at least the first experience of the sacred sacrificial meal is truly initiation (similar, though on a far higher plane, to the introduction to divine mysteries which initiation into all religion brings) —all this makes the Holy Eucharist suitable to be included among the sacraments of Christian initiation.[1]

What follows is not a treatise on the Eucharist but a consideration of it as part of the process of initiation. (For a fuller treatment of the Eucharist as part of Christian life see No. 52 of this series, *The Eucharist*.)

The third sacrament of Christian initiation, then, is the Eucharist, which is the consummation of the whole process. Baptism and confirmation exist for the Eucharist. They prepare for it and lead up to it. Christian initiation is really initiation into the Eucharistic mystery. The object and the

---

[1] This view is strongly held by Jean Danielou, and was expressed by him as early as 1952.

goal of the process of Christian initiation is to bring us to live the Eucharistic life. Baptism and confirmation depute us to worship, but that worship reaches its high point in the Eucharistic sacrifice. Only through the Eucharist are we able to offer God those "spiritual sacrifices" acceptable to him, that "spiritual service" which our baptism demands of us. Baptism and confirmation demand the Eucharist as their completion because their function is to incorporate us more perfectly into Christ, but in the Eucharist we come into direct contact with the glorious body of Christ: he abides in us and we in him. The Eucharist therefore accomplishes complete incorporation into Christ.

The bond of union among these three sacraments is the Paschal mystery, the central mystery of the Christian life. Baptism draws its power and its effectiveness from the Paschal mystery, as we have seen, but the Eucharist is the Paschal mystery made present in sign and symbol.

Both baptism and the Eucharist are Paschal sacraments, participation in Christ the risen Lord who has passed through death. But the participation in the Pasch achieved in the Eucharist is greater than that achieved in baptism, for the mystery of the dying and rising is more perfectly present in the Eucharist.

Through the Eucharist each Christian is enabled to rediscover the meaning of baptism and confirmation and the Eucharist itself. The Eucharist enables him to renew his Christian initiation, to perfect and complete it until his assimilation to Christ crucified and risen is perfect.[2]

The Fathers appreciated the relationship between baptism and the Eucharist in their baptismal catechesis. St Ambrose, for example, shows the neophyte as hastening towards the heavenly banquet: "Having laid aside the clothing of his ancient error, his youth renewed like the eagle's, he hastens towards this heavenly banquet. He arrives, and seeing the Holy Altar prepared, cries out 'You have prepared a table for me' (On the Mysteries, No. 43)."

[2] William J. O'Shea, *Sacraments of Initiation* (Englewood Cliffs, N.J.: Prentice-Hall, 1966), p. 69.

Theodore of Mopsuestia, an Eastern writer of the fourth century, explains the sacred mysteries as follows:

> In the same way as we receive the birth of baptism by means of the death of Christ, so also with our food, we receive this sacramentary by means of his death. . . . To take the oblation and participate in the mysteries is to commemorate the death of Our Lord which gains resurrection and the hope of immortality for us; for it is fitting that we who have received the sacramental birth through the death of Christ should receive the nourishment of the sacrament of immortality through the same death. We must be nourished from the same source from which we are born (Homily 15, 6).[3]

The Vatican Council also stresses the close connection:

> Nevertheless the liturgy is the summit towards which the activity of the Church is directed; at the same time it is the fountain from which all her power flows. For the goal of apostolic works is that all who are made sons of God by faith and baptism should come together to praise God in the midst of his Church, to take part in her sacrifice, and to eat the Lord's Supper (Liturgy Constitution No. 10).[4]

It is hardly possible, and still less is it desirable, to treat the Eucharist as sacrifice and sacrament separately. In recent years communion has come to be considered a part of the sacred sacrificial meal much more than it was in former times. On the other hand, there must not be such a stress on the meal element that the sacrificial element is neglected or disregarded. The Eucharist is a sacred sacrificial meal.

The consideration of the Eucharist as a sacrament of initiation has special force with regard to the first Holy Communion and participation in the Eucharistic meal, although Christian initiation in one sense is a continuing process which will never be finished until we achieve the reality of full participation in the Paschal mystery in heaven.

In the early Church, as we have seen, adults immediately after their baptism were led in procession into the assembly. During this entry, Psalm 42 (which up to the recent revision

---

[3] Quoted by R. Béraudy, "L'initiation chrétienne," in A. G. Martimort, ed., L'église en prière (Tournai: Desclée, 1965), p. 580.
[4] Walter M. Abbot, S.J., ed., The Documents of Vatican II (New York: America Press, 1966), p. 142.

of the rite of the Mass used to be recited by the priest at the foot of the altar) was sung.

Hippolytus mentions that at the time of their first communion neophytes received a mixture of milk and honey to which water was added as well as the eucharistic bread and wine. St Ambrose refers to this, and John the Deacon said milk and honey were symbols of "the land of the Resurrection," which had been promised to the Jews as a land flowing with milk and honey. By giving them to the neophytes, the Church taught the neophytes that these gifts were the object of the divine promise.

The Eucharist is the full celebration of the Paschal mystery in which baptism and the whole Paschal preparation make the initiated worthy to take part. Father Danielou sums the whole matter up when he says that we must see in baptism "the beginning of what the Eucharist brings about in all its fulness."

The custom has grown up of receiving communion before or after Mass or even outside it. Although this custom has been justified and permitted for practical reasons, it has had the bad effect of separating the meal from the sacrifice. It also gave rise to the impression that communion was something by itself, apart from the Mass. Reverence for the Real Presence and the idea of a personal contact with the Body of Christ gave this devotion a basis of sentiment which it would be irreverent and insensitive to call sentimentality. On the other hand, until recently, many people attended Mass at certain times on Sunday to fulfil their obligation when there was no communion possible at the Mass. The changes with regard to fasting laws have helped to end this custom which verged on abuse.

The Church has always made it clear that communion is an integral part of the Eucharistic sacrifice. The custom—Béraudy roundly calls it the abuse[5]—of delaying communion until after Mass started in the eleventh century. In the thirteenth century *the Episcopal Ceremonial* actually prescribed (for Easter of all days!) that if the bishop did not celebrate Mass in the cathedral, Holy Communion should be

[5] Béraudy, *op. cit.,* p. 461.

distributed at a side altar by a priest other than the celebrant before, during, and after Mass. The Roman Ritual tried to restrict this practice on the ground that "the prayers which are said after Mass are not only for the priest but also the other communicants." The Code of Canon Law and the Ritual of 1925 allowed the custom. Since the encyclical *Mediator Dei,* this custom is more reluctantly allowed.

The custom of communion outside Mass, apart from the special case of communion of the sick, developed after the Council of Trent, though not without opposition.

From the eighteenth century, this custom increased, even though liturgists kept insisting that it was not the normal thing and could be justified only with a very good reason. Numerous rituals also insisted that it was the proper thing to communicate at Mass but at the same time included a list of reasons excusing from this.

Pius XII in *Mediator Dei,* the great reforming liturgical encyclical, insisted on this teaching in a similar way. In fact, he praised those who not only received communion within the Mass but who wished to communicate with the hosts consecrated at the same Mass.

Nevertheless, *Mediator Dei* did not propose a doctrinal prohibition which would have excluded Holy Communion for those who are legitimately impeded from assisting at Mass. Hence *Mediator Dei* makes allowance for them to receive Communion before, after, or outside Mass. But it stressed (following Benedict XV) that even when Holy Communion is received apart from Mass, it keeps its relation to the Mass and is a participation in the sacrifice of the Mass.

As we have seen, the growth of this practice was the result of circumstances, some of which in modern times, are really valid excuses for departing from the ideal. But separation could not be blamed on the teaching of the Church. It was after the Council of Trent that the custom developed, but it cannot be attributed to the Council of Trent. The Council is very clear about the fact that communion is the means of participating most abundantly in the fruits of the sacrifice of the Mass. The Council states: "The holy Council would desire that in every Mass the faithful who are present communicate not only in spiritual desire, but by a sacramental reception of the Eucharist, so they might receive greater benefits from this most holy sacrifice." [6]

The Vatican Council does not say anything about communion outside the usual time, and thus leaves in force the ruling of *Mediator Dei*. However, it gives great encouragement to the practice of receiving Holy Communion at the proper time in the Mass: "Hearty endorsement is given to that closer form of participation in the Mass whereby the faithful, after the priest's communion, receive the Lord's body under elements consecrated at that very sacrifice (Liturgy Constitution" (No. 55).[7]

It would be a great pity if, for strict liturgical reasons, Holy Communion were denied to those who cannot possibly attend Mass. In modern circumstances, this may easily happen. Béraudy says:

> Still, communions separate from Mass are only to be tolerated. That is why the Church does not allow them without a reasonable cause. Today, when the law of fasting has been eased and when the faculties given to Ordinaries to authorize masses in the evening make communion within the Mass very easy, one can say that the reasons for communicating outside of Mass are less numerous than in the past.[8]

This has been a digression, but not without value. The one thing which is clear is that for adults the discipline of the early Church was quite clear: immediately after baptism they should take part in Mass and receive Holy Communion.

The Eastern Church has remained faithful to this unity of Christian initiation to the extent that even up to the present time they give Holy Communion even to newly born babies immediately after their baptism. As we have seen, this was the custom in the West up through the twelfth century. In 1215 the Council of the Lateran made communion obligatory only after the age of discretion. Incidentally, the Council of the Lateran made communion obligatory at least once a year.

[6] Denziger, *En Chéridion*, 944. See *The Church Teaches* (Documents of the Church in English Translation), St. Mary's College, Kansas (St. Louis and New York: B. Herder, 1955), No. 753, p. 294.

[7] *The Documents of Vatican II*, p. 156.

[8] Béraudy, *op. cit.*, p. 464.

This is an ecclesiastical law, no doubt a good one from a legalistic point of view. But the comments of St Ambrose are interesting; he speaks about the custom which apparently existed in the East in his day. In a sermon on the sacraments, after he has spoken about "our daily bread" in the Our Father and referred it to the Eucharist, he says: "If it is daily bread why wait a year to receive it as the Greeks do in the Orient. Receive each day what can help you each day. Live in such a way that you are worthy to receive it each day. He who is not worthy to receive it every day is not worthy to receive it after a year." [9]

After the Reformation, in some countries (for example, France) Holy Communion for children was postponed until twelve years of age. This was combined with a semi-Jansenist reverence for Holy Communion which regarded the receiving of the Body of Christ with such awe that it was the reward of virtue instead of the nourishment of the soul—and was to be received but seldom, even after first communion.

Pope Pius X's epoch-making decree of 1910 on frequent communion, *Quam Singulari,* marked the end of the Jansenistic attitude of putting off Holy Communion on account of "reverence," and restored the practice of frequent communion. With regard to children, it emphasised that this should not be regarded as the goal of their formation, to be delayed until a comparatively late age, but was to be given as soon as a child could prepare with piety for the Eucharist and was sufficiently instructed according to his age ("pro modulo suo," as the decree says, i.e., "according to their little capacity").

In case of danger of death, it is sufficient that they be able somehow to distinguish the Eucharist from ordinary bread and receive it with religious respect.

THE EUCHARIST: MEAL AND SACRIFICE

There has been a certain amount of confusion recently caused by some overstressing of the meal aspect of the Eucharist. This is a reaction against the Council of Trent's at-

[9] Sermo V, *De Sacramentis,* No. 25, quoted in Botte, *Ambroise de Milan, Des Sacraments, des Mystères* (Paris: Editions du Cerf, 1961), p. 133.

titude, which stressed the sacrifice element in an attempt to refute attacks of the Reformers.

There is a need for a synthesis of the two elements, and it is obviously far beyond the scope of this book to attempt such a synthesis. It is no reflection on Trent to suggest that its definitions do not provide the basis for a satisfactory Eucharistic theology—the members of that Council were concentrating on points which the Reformers attacked and taking for granted what was commonly accepted.

The Vatican Council's Constitution on the Liturgy, because of its magnificent synthesis of the language of Trent and the language of contemporary sacramental theology, should provide the basis for a renewed theology of the Mass that can reconcile the two schools of thought. Father Nicholas Lash maintains this to be possible in an article in the *Clergy Review*.[10]

The conclusion of Father Lash is that the two attitudes— one stressing the meal element of the Eucharist and the other the sacrificial element—are perfectly reconcilable once two points are agreed upon. The first is the fact that the Mass is one of the seven sacraments. The second is that the relationship of meal to sacrifice, within the structure of this sacrament, is that of sign to signified.

The Vatican Council, in the Constitution on the Liturgy, expressed this double element as giving the true balance:

> At the Last Supper, on the night when He was betrayed, Our Saviour instituted the Eucharistic Sacrifice of His Body and Blood. He did this in order to perpetuate the sacrifice of the Cross throughout the centuries until He should come again, and so to entrust to His beloved spouse, the Church, a memorial of his death and resurrection: a sacrament of love, a sign of unity, a bond of charity, a paschal banquet in which Christ is consumed, the mind is filled with grace, and a pledge of future glory is given to us (Liturgy Constitution No. 47).[11]

The Eucharistic sacrifice, then, is that sacrament which as effective memorial of Christ's saving death and Resurrection is the covenant—sacrifice—meal—of the new people of God. It *recalls* that covenant sealed on Calvary, it *actualises* the

[10] London, December, 1965.
[11] *The Documents of Vatican II*, p. 154.

covenant-union in the worshipping assembly (insofar as members cooperate in faith and charity), and it *anticipates* the covenant's perfect fulfilment in the eschatological Messianic banquet.

PART TWO

CHRISTIAN INITIATION AND THE CHURCH TODAY

CHAPTER VI

THIS WORLD
AND THE NEXT

Christian initiation, especially in all the impressiveness of the Paschal vigil, is so beautiful, so "out of this world," it has led the new Christian to such heights, that, as Louis Bouyer says, what follows in this world might seem only to be an anticlimax. The sacramental life to which the Christian has been initiated is so wonderful and is so strong a pledge of future glory that the material world might well tend to pale to insignificance. The Christian might well be tempted to ask in a derogatory way about mundane matters, *Quid ad aeternitatem?*—What is the value of these transitory things compared to eternity? What comparison is there between the first taste of eternal life given by the gift of the Spirit in the initiation into the wonderful mysteries of God and the ordinary concerns of everyday life, the joys and sorrows, hopes and fears, of this earthly pilgrimage? Indeed, the stronger faith is, the more there is the inclination to experience a feeling almost of unreality, or of an unwelcome reality, at having to be immersed in the things of this world.

The very beauty of the ideas and customs we have been considering with regard to the sacramental life of the Church might seem to have little relation to life as we know it. The war in Viet-Nam, the population explosion, anguished moral problems in marriage, half of God's world at near-starvation level, man's inhumanity to man, sickness, horrible diseases, our own personal sufferings: these things are the stuff of our earthly existence. But do they not seem to intrude into the beauty we have experienced? Singing the *Exsultet* in the Easter vigil—that canticle to the light of the risen Christ which is an invitation to exultant joy—in the security and happiness of a brilliantly lit church and of a beautifully staged ceremony as we enthusiastically renew our baptismal vows, are we trying to pretend that evil does not exist or that we should not think about it? Or putting it another way, how can the Christian in the midst of so much evil and suffering have the unmixed joy in the proclamation of Christ's victory to which the Church invites us?

Christians, too, have always been open to the two-fold accusation, often with good reason, that (1) because of the supreme value they put on the next life, they tend to have little concern for this life, and (2) there seems to be no real relation between the joys and ecstasies of the sacramental life and the hard realities of everyday life in the world.

However, if we are to cease regarding religion (in the words of Lenin) as "pie in the sky when you die" and being "so heavenly minded that we are no earthly good," and if we no longer wish to seek in the Church an ostrich-like retreat from the anguished problems of human life, we need a delicate balance which has not always been achieved throughout the history of Christianity.

Let us say bluntly that there have been ages—our own has been one—when there was too much concentration on the things of the other world, to the detriment of the things of this world.[1] Religion can be, and should be, a source of comfort amid the hardships and sorrows of this life, but it does not dull their impact or make us feel them the less, acting as a spiritual anaesthetic. To take a simple example: to hope with confidence that a loved one has gone to heaven and even to be glad about that aspect of a bereavement does not dispel for the widow the aching void left by such a loss, nor does it make the task of rearing children alone any easier. To give only spiritual comfort to a bereaved person, especially in the first throes of his grief and anxiety, not only

---

[1] See the Pastoral Constitution, *Gaudium et Spes, The Church in the World of Today,* No. 43, in Walter M. Abbot, S.J., *The Documents of Vatican II* (New York: America Press, 1966), p. 243.

betrays a lack of knowledge of human nature but goes against the pattern of Our Lord's own example.

Too much concentration on the things of the spirit can even lead to an inhuman insensitivity which is the opposite of love; by a strange paradox, it can even lead to the tolerating of injustice and evil. An example of such an attitude readily springs to mind. In nineteenth-century England, there was far greater—and I believe genuine—interest in and practice of religion than there is now; yet this was an age of monstrous social injustice towards the working class. Some who praised God on Sunday were guilty of crimes, during the rest of the week (crimes that cried to heaven for vengeance). Even the Church was slow to make its voice felt against these evils, while religious controversy raged apace.

Nevertheless, authentic Christianity is not world-fleeing. In the early Church, the very Christian who thrilled to his initiation into the happiness of the Christian assembly might well be condemning himself to the harsh brutalities of the Roman arena on the morrow.

In fact, although Christianity is a religion of joy and hope because Christ the Saviour has risen as the symbol of our own rising, nevertheless the Church never lets us forget the means by which he achieved that redemption: struggle, suffering, and humiliation. And he is the model of the Christian who reaches the heavenly goal (which Christ has merited for him) by passing through and overcoming, with Christ's help, the "mystery of evil." And evil always remains fundamentally a mystery, obscure and dark and full of anguish, lightened by some rays of light which the love of Christ has shed on it, but a problem constantly torturing the mind and bruising the heart.

And so the Vatican Council has no glib, patronising words as it confronts the human scene: it realistically embraces the sorrows as well as the joys of mankind. The Pastoral Constitution, *Gaudium et Spes,* opens with this statement:

> The joys and hopes, the griefs and anxieties of the men of this age, especially those who are poor or in any way afflicted, these too are the joys and hopes, the griefs and anxieties of the followers of Christ. Indeed, nothing genuinely human fails

to raise an echo in their hearts. For theirs is a community composed of men. United in Christ, they are led by the Holy Spirit in their journey to the kingdom of their Father and they have welcomed the news of salvation which is meant for every man. That is why this community realises that it is truly and intimately linked with mankind and its history.

Hence this Second Vatican Council, having probed more profoundly into the mystery of the Church, now addresses itself without hesitation, not only to the sons of the Church and to all who invoke the name of Christ, but to the whole of humanity. For the Council yearns to explain to everyone how it conceives of the presence and activity of the Church in the world of today.

Therefore, the Council focuses its attention on the world of men, the whole human family along with the sum of those realities in the midst of which that family lives. It gazes upon that world which is the theatre of man's history, and carries the marks of his energies, his tragedies, and his triumphs; that world which the Christian sees as created and sustained by its Maker's love, fallen indeed into the bondage of sin, yet emancipated now by Christ. He was crucified and rose again to break the stranglehold of personified Evil, so that this world might be fashioned anew according to God's design and reach its fulfilment (Nos. 1 and 2).[2]

The whole document gives the lie to the idea that the belief of the Church and Christians in the life to come should weaken their interest in this life, make them indifferent to life's real tasks, and cause them not only to despair of temporal salvation, but to lose interest in it completely.

The Council strikes that delicate balance which is so difficult to achieve between this life and the next, between heavenly worship and earthly concern, between the claims of the secular city and the rights of the city of God. To trace the details of this balance, one would need to study many of the Council documents, but perhaps one of the best summaries of this balance is to be found in *Gaudium et Spes*.

After saying, "We are taught that God is preparing a new dwelling place and a new earth where justice will abide and whose blessedness will answer and surpass all the longings for peace which spring up in the human heart," the document goes on: "Therefore, while we are warned that it

[2] *Ibid.*, pp. 199–200.

profits a man nothing if he gain the whole world and lose himself, the expectation of a new earth must not weaken but rather stimulate our concern for cultivating this one" (No. 39).[3]

The kind of spirituality which preaches detachment from earthly things in the sense of not being interested in them—as if they were a distraction preventing one from concentrating on the things of God—is not an authentic Biblical spirituality. It is not the kind of spirituality that God wants or to which the Church invites us. There is a popular Sunday newspaper in England which claims, "All human life is there" (although often it concentrates on the seamier side of it); this could and should be claimed with more truth for the Bible and for the Church.

It appears to be a paradox that the Church can regard the next life as all-important, and consider sacramental life (which is a foretaste of it) so vital, yet at the same time give greater value to this life. The key to this paradox is the intimate connection between this life and the next.

Some have asked the question, Must we admit that the Christian belief in eternal life does indeed rob this life of meaning and discourage efforts to secure the reign of justice or simply a reduction of human suffering? The answer is definitely no. Of course, as Bouyer points out,[4] the Christian who is true to his baptism, and to Christ, with whom every celebration of the Eucharist puts him in contact anew, only lives for the full flowering in eternity of the realities lying beneath the surface of the sacramental world. To seek to deny this is to deceive others or else oneself.

But the real question is how the Christian is to strive towards that blossoming of the realities of his faith, which are only given to him in this life under the veil of the sacraments. In other words, what are the implications here and now of that loyalty to Christ which is, for us, the *sine qua non* of eternal life?

First of all, does it involve even the slightest devaluation of

---

[3] *Ibid.*, p. 237.

[4] Louis Bouyer, *Christian Initiation* (London: Burns & Oates, 1960), p. 114.

this life and, in particular, of the purely human tasks which it imposes upon us?

Nothing could be farther from the truth. Eternal life is only promised to the Christian on condition that he makes a right use of this life. He will be judged, not by the faculty he has shown for escaping from his human tasks and responsibilities, but, on the contrary, according to the fresh meaning which he has discovered in them and the renewed devotion with which he has discharged them.

If eternal life were independent of this life, then the latter would become worthless and unimportant. But that is not the case at all; Christianity knows no other eternal life but the one we prepare for, and even to some extent make, during the course of this life. Such a view of eternal life, far from nullifying this one, gives it infinite value. If this present life were due to stop tomorrow, with no hope of an afterlife, it could never have the importance conferred on every minute of it by the Christian prospect, the prospect not just of eternity but of eternal judgment and resurrection. The Christian view simply emphasises the extreme urgency of the need for every Christian to practice perfect charity. It means that he must constantly try to live in that love which is the love shown to him by God, the love which is the life of God. That love, charity, the "agape" of the Gospels, is, it should be recalled, the creative love, the love that gives and therefore gives itself. It is the love that extends to all beings and, in them, to the whole being. For once again Christianity does not know, or rather rejects, the false spirituality which neglects or condemns the body, to the benefit of the soul. When he loves souls, the Christian loves the whole man, body and soul, and devotes himself in the most realistic fashion to the well-being of the body as well as to that of the soul.[5]

The eschatological hope of the Christian—the belief that we are on our way to our true home, where our human life will finally take its full meaning, "where God will wipe the tears from our eyes," where we will rejoice not only in the triumph of the risen and glorified Christ but in our own resurrection and glorification, which we share because his

[5] Ibid., p. 114.

victory over death makes our victory possible—this hope
emphasises the need to "redeem the time," to make our pil-
grim journey a worthy one on the model of Our Lord, who
has gone before to prepare a place for us and who will re-
quire us to pass a test of love before we enter in. At the
conclusion of his eschatological discourse at the Last Supper,
Our Lord puts this test in very concrete terms:

> Then the King will say to those on his right hand, "Come,
> you whom my Father has blessed, take for your heritage the
> kingdom prepared for you since the foundation of the world.
> For I was hungry and you gave me food; I was thirsty and
> you gave me drink; I was a stranger and you made me wel-
> come; naked and you clothed me, sick and you visited me,
> in prison and you came to see me." Then the virtuous will
> say to him in reply, "Lord, when did we see you hungry and
> feed you; or thirsty and give you drink? When did we see
> you a stranger and made you welcome; naked and clothe you;
> sick or in prison and go to see you?" And the King will answer,
> "I tell you solemnly, in so far as you did this to one of the
> least of these brothers of mine, you did it to me" (Mark
> 25:34–40).

Love which is shown by deeds is our passport to our
heavenly country. And so their very eschatological hope
makes extremely urgent the need for Christians to practise as
perfect a love as they can.

(There is an ancient Sacramentary which illustrates this
point very well and points to the true mind of the Church.
Instead of the usual dismissal at the end of the Eucharistic
assembly—*Ite missa est,* so difficult to translate—it has
something like this: *Ite et extendite amorem erga fratres
vestros*—"Go and show love to your brethren".) Christians
know from the parable of the Good Samaritan who their
brethren are: every human being of whatever race, colour,
creed or nation. These words make explicit the whole message
of the Eucharist, of the liturgy, of Christianity itself.

The love we are supposed to show is not a vague, senti-
mental, sterile love which warms itself on the glow of self-
righteousness gained by "feeling good" about others and
their sufferings. It is not an abstract love which shrinks to
come into contact with the harsh and sometimes dirty reali-

ties of life. It is not the sort of love which thinks a Christian or a priest or religious should not "get involved." What a Spanish bishop said so beautifully during the Council about priests can apply to all Christians: "The consecrated hands of a priest do not get soiled by binding up the wounds of suffering humanity."

The love to which our initiation and our vocation as Christians calls us is a genuine, concrete, committed love on the model of Christ himself, which does not divide the world into persons and causes "suitable" for our love and those which are not or believe that Christians and priests should only be concerned with "nice things," that they should not risk their salvation by coming into close contact with evil, that they should withdraw when any spiritual danger looms or the disapproval of the world gets too great.

It is a love which does not arbitrarily regard certain activities as holy and becoming and others, equally good in their own way, as somehow unfitting. Perhaps I may be forgiven for using a personal example to show what I mean. After I had finished the other book I wrote in this series, World Poverty and the Christian, a very good Catholic of my acquaintance said to me, "It is very nice your writing these books, but what a pity you are not a *real* priest, hearing confessions, preaching, giving the Sacraments!"

This Catholic was echoing the fallacy that only in Church can we really honour God and that the priest's place is only in the sanctuary and the sacristy.

The parable of the Good Samaritan comes to mind again with our Lord's own warning against a false dichotomy in our lives.

We all have been brought up to look down on the unfeeling priest and the Levite in the parable, and rightly so, but what must their point of view have been? They were coming down from Jerusalem, after taking part in the worship of the people of God, the liturgical action which, for them, was the high point of their service of God; possibly they were deep in conversation about those ceremonies or were discussing, as Biblical scholars, the scriptural lore which they had heard read out. The plight of the man beaten by robbers, lying half dead on the roadside, must have seemed an unwelcome intrusion, a distraction from the things of God, the things that *really* mattered. By intervening, they might get involved in an unsavoury, perhaps a dangerous incident, if the bandits were still about, and in any case, it would mean delaying their journey and going to an awful lot of trouble; their priestly dignity might be jeopardised. It was much better to leave the whole sordid business to some unspiritual person like an heretical Samaritan. Of course, from their own point of view, they were quite right—however, Our Lord did not agree with them.

There is not space here to treat at great length of the relation between liturgy and life or between the Christian and the problems of this world. This has been done in the majestic pastoral Constitution, *Gaudium et Spes*—the longest document of the Council, which ranks with the Constitution on the Church as the most important document of the Council. It is a solemn declaration by the Church in Council of the Church's love and concern for the world, that world of which the scriptures say, "God loved the world so much that he gave his only son . . . that through Him the world might be saved" (John 3:6–17)—and at what a cost!

Christian initiation brings with it then, the obligation to love the world and to be interested in and work for the solution of its problems. It was this love which motivated the Council fathers to spend so much time seeking a dialogue with the world in the lengthy discussions which are summarised in *Gaudium et Spes*, in keeping with the spirit of Pope John and following the exhortation of Pope Paul in his first encyclical, *Ecclesiam Suam* (6th August 1964). This remarkable encyclical has a sentence which summarises the dominant theme of the Church in the modern world and which translates Christian love into terms the world can understand and appreciate and which is far from the spirit of fleeing from the world: "All things human are our concern. We share with the whole of humanity a common nature, human life (No. 54)."

In a commentary on *Gaudium et Spes*, Canon F. Houtart,

after describing the reasons why the Council spoke to the
whole of mankind, says:

> For the People of God, who are called to give witness to the
> message of the Lord, this is of fundamental importance. For
> it is precisely according to the extent to which we relate to the
> world that we shall be capable of fulfilling this our mission,
> as layman or priest, as deacon or bishop, as individuals or as
> a community, as the Universal Church or as a local Church.[6]

Insofar, then, as the Church and members of it have rejected the world, they have been false to the mission of
Christianity. The Council implicitly admits that the "religionless Christianity" which is a fashion, if not a feature of our
age, to say nothing of some forms of atheism (see Art. 19,
20, 21), can be traced, in part, to aloofness or hostility on
the part of Christians towards the human problems and
values of this world.

The life of the Church, then, the liturgy itself, and Christian initiation, must be linked to life, life as lived in this
world. *Gaudium et Spes,* following Pope John in *Mater et
Magistra,* makes this very clear in one passage:

> This Council exhorts Christians, as citizens of two cities, to
> strive to discharge their earthly duties conscientiously and in
> response to the gospel spirit. They are mistaken who, knowing
> that we have here no abiding city but seek one which is to
> come, think that they may therefore shirk their earthly re-
> sponsibilities. For they are forgetting that by the faith itself
> they are more than ever obliged to measure up to these duties,
> each according to his proper vocation. Nor, on the contrary,
> are they any less wide of the mark who think that religion
> consists in acts of worship alone and in the discharge of certain
> moral obligations, and who imagine they can plunge them-
> selves into earthly affairs in such a way as to imply that these
> are altogether divorced from the religious life. This split be-
> tween the faith which many profess and their daily lives de-
> serves to be counted among the more serious errors of our
> age. Long since, the prophets of the Old Testament fought
> vehemently against this scandal and even more so did Jesus

---

[6] Canon F. Houtart, "The Historical and Sociological Background
of the Constitution *Gaudium et Spes*" in a symposium-commentary
The Church in the Modern World, edited by the present writer and
to be published by Benziger, New York.

Christ Himself in the New Testament threaten it with grave punishments.

Therefore, let there be no false opposition between professional and social activities on the one part, and religious life on the other. The Christian who neglects his temporal duties neglects his duties toward his neighbour and even God, and jeopardises his eternal salvation.[7]

This chapter has been an introduction, a necessary one I believe, to the consideration of how Christian initiation can be made meaningful in modern life, in the life of the twentieth century, in "Christian" countries and those still looked on as mission regions with their civilisations and cultures as yet untouched by Christianity.

[7] *The Documents of Vatican II,* pp. 242–43.

CHAPTER VII

CHRISTIAN INITIATION
TO THE PRESENT DAY

In the first part of the book we have seen how the practises of the early Church with regard to Christian initiation came gradually to be modified, without being completely adapted to new conditions, especially after the sixth century, when infant baptism became the rule.

These modifications not only affected the rites of the sacraments of initiation but also caused a revision in the whole process of learning to be a Christian.

As we have seen, in the early Church there was a strict and lengthy doctrinal moral and spiritual formation in preparation for the sacraments. The catechesis was Biblical and was linked to prayer and fasting.

Once infant baptism became common, the preparation for the sacraments was superseded by the teaching of doctrine and training in Christian living given when the child had reached the age to profit by it. In the Middle Ages, this was conveyed by ordinary preaching, by the whole Christian atmosphere, of the civilisation, by the pictorial instruction given by the very walls, pictures and stained glass of the cathedrals and churches, by the special treatises written on theology and religion, especially in the twelfth, thirteenth and fourteenth centuries. As the whole society was a Christian one and children were baptised shortly after they were born, the religious training of children, their conscious initiation into Christian living at an age when they could profit by it, took place at school, in church and in the family.

The question of ordinary education—as distinct from

university education—and religious instruction has been very much neglected by historians. Nevertheless, from the scattered and rather fragmentary evidence, it is possible to assert that by the twelfth century a system of schools right down to rural elementary level had been established in which religious instruction was given and other subjects were taught through religious texts.

There was not that clear-cut distinction between the religious and other school subjects which we are accustomed to. Religion permeated secular branches of learning, even elementary biology and other sciences. For example, reading was taught by reading the Psalter. The Middle Ages were religiously oriented to a remarkable extent. Religion and life were so intimately connected that a special subject for religious instruction as such would have seemed almost superfluous.

It is interesting to note that in the Middle Ages there were no catechisms: first of all because oral teaching was the rule when books were so difficult to produce and to come by, and also because teachers went to the sacred scripture for their teaching. From the twelfth century onwards translations of the Bible into the vernacular became common.

Moreover, religious instruction was more a question of formation than of mere information. The pupils of even the elementary schools were taught to sing the psalms and take an active part in the worship of the Church.

Religious training in the family was linked in an essentially practical way to this participation. In the houses of the nobles, there was always a chapel and a chaplain whose duty was to give religious (and generally) secular education. Even for children outside this orbit, there was the parish church where the child could take part in the ceremonies, listen to sermons, watch and take part in religious dramas, morality plays, etc.

With regard to children with Jewish or Moslem parents who were converted, special arrangements were made. A special teacher was set aside for their religious instruction.

There was a considerable outburst of missionary activity in the thirteenth and fourteenth centuries. Indeed, St Thomas

Acquinas wrote his philosophical work, *Summa Contra Gentiles,* to be the ammunition for the apologetics of the Dominican and Franciscan friars in their missionary endeavours. The intellectual, philosophical approach is marked. And the rites of initiation were in the form which had developed in Europe. For example, John of Montecorvino, at the beginning of the fourteenth century in China, was obviously introducing Western religious customs into that flourishing, but short-lived mission to the Chinese, as can be seen by the two letters written by him from Peking.

The decline of religion at the end of the Middle Ages and the break-up of the unity of Christendom changed the whole situation, and naturally this affected the Christian initiation of those born into the Catholic faith. Not only did religious controversy come to the fore, but gradually society became more secular.

When the Council of Trent met in the middle of the sixteenth century with the two-fold purpose of opposing the teachings of the Reformation and attempting the reform of the Church, one of its main tasks and achievements was to compile a catechism: *The Catechism of the Council of Trent.* Although this was affected by the general aims of the Council and had much of a correct but negative aspect, in many ways it had great positive values. It was, of course, a far bigger and deeper theological work than we normally understand by the word "catechism." However, this did not become, unfortunately, the basis of the catechisms which were generally used in the centuries following Trent. The more polemical, intellectual and rather legalistic catechisms of Peter Canisius and others became the main doctrinal weapon of the Counter-Reformation. They were suitable for the "siege mentality" which developed in the Church as she saw herself attacked on all sides, first by the Reformers, then by the rationalists of the eighteenth-century enlightenment and anti-religious elements of the French Revolution, then by the materialism and scientific agnosticism of the nineteenth century.

Religious instruction of children in the Catholic countries of Europe was based on these catechetical compendia and often consisted of learning by heart complicated, abstract formulae which hardly reached the mind and certainly did not touch the heart. This has continued to our own day. For example, the definition of "God" which I learned before I was ten from the English catechism was: "God is the supreme spirit who alone exists of Himself and is infinite in all perfections." A "sacrament" was defined as "an outward sign of inward grace by which grace is given to the soul"; this definition is perfectly true, but it conveys the idea that sacraments are just things, sacred things indeed, but still things.

It would be easy to list the many defects in such catechesis until the catechetical renewal of the present century (indeed of the last twenty-five years) got under way.

In the sixteenth and seventeenth centuries, there was a great expansion of missionary activity of a more enduring and systematic kind than that of the thirteenth and fourteenth centuries which the Franciscans and Dominicans had promoted.

This expansion followed in the wake of Portuguese and Spanish explorations and colonisation. There is not space here to describe at length this missionary activity from the point of view of the history of the missions.[1] But it is important to see the place given to Christian initiation in this Christian expansion in the new worlds of West and East which were being opened up to European colonisation.[2]

From the end of the sixteenth century to the present day, the theory with regard to Christian initiation, especially with regard to preparation for baptism, was strict. In his *Historia Ecclesiastica Indiana,* a description of the beginnings of the missions of Latin America, written at the end of the sixteenth century, Fray Geronimo de Mendieta has lengthy chapters on the celebration of baptism and speaks of the grave responsibility of missionaries in the conferring of baptism; this was,

[1] Two books in this series do this: R. C. de Lavignette, *Christianity and Colonialism,* and Bernard de Vaulx, *History of Missions.*

[2] I do not know of a good treatment in English of this. A very useful summary is contained in "L'initiation et la celebration baptismale dans les missions du 16e siècle à nos jours," by I. Beckman in *Du Catechumát à la Confirmation,* Symposium, La Maison-Dieu No. 58 (Paris: Editions du Cerf, 1959).

on the whole, the theoretical attitude of the whole epoch from the time of the great discoveries, right up to our day. In 1930, a missionary in China wrote: "Every missionary should consider baptismal water as sacred as the Eucharist and should be prudent in baptising." However, there was often, especially in the early days, a considerable gulf between theory and practice, and even when this strict observance was respected, attempts at adaptation of rites to indigenous culture and mentalities were rare, with some notable, but not very successful exceptions.

Nevertheless, to characterise the Spanish-Portuguese missionary methods of the sixteenth century as forced baptisms and mass conversions is far too sweeping a generalisation. Even when there was evangelisation at the sword's point, as indeed there was at first, a practice not completely abolished until the reign of Philip II in the second half of the century, conversion did have some kind of religious instruction as its basis, given first of all through interpreters and then in the different native languages when they had been learnt by the missionaries. The Franciscans, according to Robert Ricard, insisted that the administration of baptism should always be preceded by instruction, more or less summary according to circumstances.[3] Even as early as the third decade of the sixteenth century in Mexico, a handful of missionaries baptised 5,000 pagans, but gave them instruction first and even a certain catechesis before baptism.

In the East also, there was a consciousness of the necessity of preparation. The first Augustinian (Portuguese) missionaries to the Philippines baptised only about a hundred pagans in the six years after their arrival in 1564. It was only after an intense study of the language, after missionary work was consolidated, that the number of baptisms began to increase.

Various Councils in South America, such as the Council of Lima (1552) and of Quito (1570)—and there were similar examples in the East—testified to the necessity of a period of instruction.

Nevertheless, the Portuguese and Spanish missions did not,

[3] Robert Ricard, *La conquête spirituelle du Mexique* (Paris: 1938), p. 105.

in all probability, have anything that would be regarded as a catechumenate and there was no uniformity with regard to the period of instruction. On the whole, we can say that the preparation for baptism was often far too short and superficial. The need for instruction was realised. However, the sheer physical pressure of numbers on a handful of missionaries and the current ideas of the importance of baptism for salvation to save the souls of the heathen, "with which hell is being daily filled" (according to the prayer of St Francis Xavier), often meant a great stress on numbers of baptisms and extensive, rather than intensive preparation. For example, St Francis himself baptised in the month of December (1543) alone 10,000 pagans!

In the seventeenth century in China, missionaries proceeded with much more caution and slowness. Although this was not always the case in Brazil and Africa in general, nevertheless the Jesuits, in their missions, did introduce something more than mere summary instruction.

The foundation of the *Congregatio de Propaganda Fide* in 1622 gave an impetus to a more systematic preparation for baptism, but by the eighteenth century the directives from the Congregation had a retarding effect on those initiatives which had begun even in the sixteenth century to respect pagan customs and to adapt them.

The traditional baptismal occasions of the Church, Easter and Pentecost, were done away with since they could not be observed by pagans. Other directives insisted, in accord with the spirit of the times, as we already noted, on detailed instruction in Christian doctrine and the abolition of anything reminiscent of pagan rites, especially the cult of ancestors.[4] This latter emphasis was due to the Chinese missionaries, who had by then, subsequent to the Chinese Rites affair, departed from the understanding attitude of the early seventeenth-century Chinese missionaries towards ancestor worship. This

---

[4] The Directives were first published in the form of *Instructiones* in 1669 at Prague and then at Rome in 1744, and after 1840 became known as *Monita ad Missionarios Sacrae Congregationis de Propaganda Fide*.

case is too well known to dwell on, but as it is so relevant to our subject it is worth considering briefly.

Father Matteo Ricci was a Jesuit who went to China in 1583 to introduce Christianity. He made himself very acceptable to the Chinese because he was a scholar who studied their literature and was able to dispute with their learned men —the Mandarins—and also was a learned mathemetician who sought contact with those of the Far East. Because of his friendship with some of the Mandarins, brought about by his attitude (indeed, he baptised several of them), he was received in Peking in 1601 and acquired some land there. He wrote a number of books on religion and also some scientific works which enhanced his reputation for scholarship. His great principle, following St Francis Xavier, was that it was possible to remain a good Chinese and at the same time become a good Christian. His mission was successful, and by the time of his death in 1610 he had baptised 2,000 Chinese. He was firmly convinced that traditional Chinese rites such as the honours paid to ancestors and to Confucius were certainly not idolatrous and perhaps not superstitious. His attitude of toleration towards these rites had no doubt been a factor in his success, but it also gave rise to a quarrel with other missionaries over the rites. In 1631 two missionaries came from Manila, one a Franciscan called Father Antonio de Santa Maria and the other Father Moralles, a Dominican. They believed in abolishing completely any connection between Christianity and paganism and completely distrusted rites of pagan religions. They became fierce opponents of the method of adaptation adopted by Father Ricci. The dispute dragged on for a long time, but in 1742 the Pope gave a complete and definitive condemnation of the rites and thus reversed the policy of the early Chinese missionaries. By this time a persecution of the Christians had taken place under the Emperor Kang 'Hi because he insisted that the missionaries must seek permission if they wished to reside in China, and this permission would only be given to those who were prepared to act like Father Ricci.

There was also a good deal of difficulty with regard to the

formation of native clergy. By the beginning of the eighteenth century, priests of the Paris Foreign Missions Society had acquired a good deal of influence and had succeeded in having a number of Chinese ordained. They were, however, completely against the policy of Father Ricci and they had a good deal of influence on Propaganda.

Another notable case with regard to local customs concerned Father Robert de Nobili, S.J. In India the Portuguese missionaries had come up against the caste system, which was a religious, and social system. It was a rigid separation of classes, and to leave a particular caste or class meant that a person was an outcast and had no position in society. The Portuguese as colonisers disregarded this system, and because it seemed so contrary to Christianity, the missionaries had no regard for it. In a way, therefore, the Portuguese brought down the caste system in a few areas where their rule was effective. Elsewhere throughout India the caste system remained in vigour and Indian Christian converts became, to all intents and purposes, Portuguese and were despised and looked upon as renegades. Not only that, but the missionaries, true to the Christian teaching of the universal brotherhood of man, antagonised Indians by being in contact with all castes. This was very much against the Indian mentality and social customs whereby contact with a member of an inferior caste automatically involved a state of grave ritual impurity.

Father de Nobili, an Italian Jesuit, arrived in India at the beginning of the seventeenth century at Madura. He realised that in that area the Jesuits had failed completely. He tried to adapt to the caste system and studied the secrets of Hinduism. He had considerable contact with the Brahmins, the highest caste, and discussed religion with them and he himself adopted the external customs of the caste. At the same time he became convinced that not all the caste customs were to be condemned and that some of them were purely civil and social and could be tolerated. This caused scandal among many of the missionaries, and he was denounced to Rome. Gregory XV in 1623 gave a decision in de Nobili's favour and, as Bernard de Vaulx wrote, "the new method of adapation thus allowed Indians to enter the Mystical Body without renouncing all their rites and traditions, in a word, without incurring the shameful name of 'renegade.' "[5]

However, in 1704, the decision given in Father de Nobili's case was reversed by Mgr Maillard de Tournon, a legate sent from Rome to enquire into the Chinese rites. Fr de Britto, S.J., and other Jesuits had pursued the policy of Fr de Nobili in Malabar; their attitude had been denounced by French Capuchins as showing too much toleration towards Malabar rites. Ricci and de Nobili had shown an enlightened sense of the need for adaptation and pre-evangelisation (as also had St Francis Xavier—his approach in Japan was far different from that in India). The condemnation of their ideas meant the failure of a brave attempt to present Christianity freed from the accretions of Western civilisation and culture, an attempt which would have allow a specifically Chinese and Indian Christianity to develop. We are only recently getting back to their ideas under the influence of enlightened missiologists and because of the impetus of indigenous hierarchies.

Without going into history of other missionary regions, one can say that up to the nineteenth century real adaptation to local customs was not common and was opposed by Propaganda, and a uniform system of instruction for converts had not been set up. The traditional catechumenate had not been established and the ancient traditional stages and ceremonies leading up to baptism had been ignored.

However, the ancient practice of the catechumenate in the Church was restored toward the end of the nineteenth century in the vast missionary territories of Africa. The first missionaries in Africa in the nineteenth century, the Holy Ghost Fathers, were instructed by the Venerable Father Libermann, to concentrate their attention on a serious instruction and preparation for catechumens. Cardinal Lavigerie, the founder of the White Fathers, followed this example and became the real restorer of the ancient catechumenate.

In 1878 he sent a memorandum to Cardinal Franchi of Propaganda outlining his principles with regard to the question of the catechumenate and got from him an approval

[5] Bernard de Vaulx, *op. cit.,* p. 95.

of the project and permission to go ahead with it. Lavigerie's idea was, by strictly organising the catechumenate, to prevent the falling away of converts which has always been a problem for missionaries, and also to offer a source of support and help to his converts who were full of good will but rather weak. He wrote to his missionaries:

> You must explain that there are two kinds of Christians: those who believe in our Lord without being baptised, who are called "catechumens," and those who are baptised and are called the "faithful." You must explain that you cannot admit all to the ranks of the "faithful," and consequently to baptism, but you can admit only those who have the courage to practise completely. . . . With regard to the others who are doubtful of themselves, or who cannot bring themselves to renounce their bad customs, you can only admit them to the catechumenate; on this account they are already Christians, it is true, but they cannot be baptised until they renounce everything, (opposed to Christianity) and this may only be at the time of death.[6]

Lavigerie introduced three stages in the catechumenate. The first stage included those who were just beginning, whom he called "postulants" according to the name which they had in the early Church. These had shown a serious desire for baptism and Christianity with its duties and rites. According to the ancient "discipline of the secret," participation in Mass and public worship was not yet allowed to them, and for doctrinal instruction they were given a reduced course in certain truths of the moral law and Christian life. The second group, which included real catechumens, were to be initiated by a considerable increase in the truths which they were taught, including the specifically Christian truths of the Trinity, the Incarnation of Christ, the means of grace and salvation of the Church, and during Holy Mass should be admitted to the Liturgy of the Word, the old Mass of the Catechumens. In the third group were those who were "chosen" or "elect," and they could commence their immediate preparation for baptism.

For reasons of prudence and local circumstances, in Africa the Cardinal provided for at least four years of catechu-

---

[6] Lavigerie quoted St Augustine to justify this distinction.

menate, two years as postulants and two years for the catechumenate itself.

The White Fathers have kept substantially to this custom
to this day. This rule of Cardinal Lavigerie had salutory
influence on the deepening and improvement of preparation
for baptism in other African missions. Nevertheless, customs
varied in different missions and even now there is no uniformity with regard to this fundamental point of missionary
activity.

With regard to the actual liturgy of the administration of
baptism, the baptism was conferred in mission territories
according to the Roman rite from the sixteenth century
onwards. However, on account of numbers and physical conditions and also because Rome insisted on all the ceremonies
and prayers of the Roman Ritual (some of which, at times,
were completely unsuitable in local circumstances), the custom gradually grew up, in spite of prohibition, of using for the
baptism of adults the ritual for children. It can therefore be
said that by the end of the nineteenth century, this had become
the general practice in missions throughout the world, so
that now the great majority of missionaries baptise adults
according to the rite for the baptism of children, without
hesitation and without scruple of any kind. This has been a
very unfortunate development which, as we have already
noted, one can hope will be reversed by the latest decisions
of Rome and by the influence of the Liturgy Constitution.

One of the greatest disadvantages of that system was that
modern missionaries, who after all, were men of their time,
had until very recently lost the community feeling and
mentality with regard to the baptism of adults, which was
often administered almost secretly and as quickly as possible.
As I have said, it is only under the influence of the liturgical
renewal in these last years that attempts are being made to
restore the liturgical and pastoral significance of the sacrament of baptism.

From all we have said, then, it will be seen that developments both in the Christian countries of the West and in
mission territories throughout the world suffered from the
many defects in catecesis which were mentioned at the be-

ginning of this chapter. It is, of course, true, that the great truths of religion were taught and that many devout, good, committed Catholics were produced by the old system in mission territories, as well as in Europe—and some of them have suffered and died heroically for their faith. The missionary pioneers who blazed the trail for the missionary revival, often amid incredible difficulties, were men full of love of God and devotion to the Church. They were products of the old system. The grace of God and the individuality of human personality often offset the disadvantages of learning religion in the way it was then taught.

But this does not detract from the tremendous riches that have come to the Church through the catechetical, liturgical and Biblical renewal and the vista that is being opened up for more meaningful Christian initiation, especially in those countries outside Europe and the United States.

The Vatican Council has ended the period of the defensive mentality and the stress on intellectualism. A deeper insight into the nature of the Church as the people of God, a spirit of collaboration and dialogue instead of hostility towards those formerly regarded as "opponents," the return to Biblical and Patristic sources to make religion a living thing rather than a system of theological and philosophical truths—all these things, as well as specific liturgical changes, have had and will have a profound effect on the process of making new Christians and instructing those born to the faith.

Nevertheless, as we shall see, the unique mission of the Church to spread knowledge of God's truth has not been weakened by these new insights. Because the simplistic attitude of St Francis Xavier towards the salvation of the heathen has been modified and the value of the culture of "anonymous" Christians has been recognised, the urgency of the essentially missionary apostolate has not been lessened. On the contrary, the more we understand the "mystery" of the Church the more we shall wish to bring the good news to all men whom God wills to be saved *and* brought to the knowledge of the truth.

Christian initiation at the present day must confront four main situations from both a catechetical and liturgical standpoint. It must decide how to approach and deal with (1) adult converts in Christian and post-Christian societies of the West, (2) the adult converts in missionary countries, (3) the catechetical instruction and liturgical training of those who are born Catholics, and (4) the catechetical instruction and liturgical training of children born Catholics in "missionary" countries.

The rites of initiation bring home one important truth which is of value for our times, perhaps of greater value for our time than at any other period, especially with regard to the countries of the West, with their Christian or post-Christian modes of thought. Namely: how impossible it is to regard the Christian religion as a body of philosophical or intellectual or cultural truths.

The Church is a unique society of a unique kind, the society of the people of God who were drawn into existence by the revelation and action of God—an action, like all actions of God, surrounded with mystery but of which the main lines are clearly to be seen.

Without any merit of his own, but not without his own efforts, a convert embraces a faith which is presented to him by a living reality—the Church—which goes back in God's plan to the beginning of Biblical times, and more specifically, to the New Testament and the age of the apostles.

Once a person is assured that God has revealed his saving design for mankind, he must give the commitment of his whole person in response to this revelation. He must, aided by God, who makes the first step in any encounter, embrace a way of life, and not merely give intellectural assent to a body of truths. The assent is, of course, necessary, but it does not come as the logical end of a process of rationalisation and evidence about the content of these truths, a process such as modern man is used to.

For this reason, attempts to bring Christianity up to date by making it completely acceptable to modern man, by making it contemporary, by making it "relevant" need to proceed with caution. It is not a question of seeing how much modern man will accept and trimming one's doctrines accordingly, nor is it a case, for example, of presenting

Christian morality as what a majority of "good" modern people are prepared to go along with (regarding the Holy Spirit as a sort of divine sociologist always on the side of the 51 per cent).

A religionless Christianity in the more extreme sense, in spite of the good will of those who have thought it up and the mystical experience of some of its best exponents such as Martin Bonhoeffer, is a contradiction in terms, as Thomas Merton has shown so lucidly in *Redeeming the Time*. It is not a Biblical Christianity, it is not the Christianity of tradition, it is not the Christianity into which the baptised were initiated. Maybe it is the only Christianity that modern man —or certain types of modern man—will accept. But this is not what Christianity is about. Paradoxically, religionless Christianity is a religion but it is not Christianity.

Of course, the taunt of Voltaire is always true to a certain extent: man does make God in his own image and the attempts of Dr Robinson and others are praiseworthy in their desire to purify the idea of God and make it acceptable to modern man. But an even worse mistake is to make religion tailor-made to what modern man himself desires. A religion such as that is man-made, and bears no relation to the uniqueness of the Christian religion, which, if it is anything, is God-made, based on a revelation which is accepted, not because it fits in with current ideas, nor because it suits a particular age, but because it comes from God. It is Christocentric or it is nothing.

There is not space to develop this theme at length. Obviously, these remarks are not intended for those who wish to present the words of God, revelation, the sacraments themselves, in language understood by modern man and in terms which are meaningful in his philosophy. Nor am I suggesting that we should forget that the grain of mustard has grown into a tree and that it is a futile process to attempt to return without discretion to all the ideas and practices of Old Testament times or those of the early Christian centuries in catechesis or in liturgy.

But in order to appreciate the riches of Christian initiation one must go back to sources, and in order to adapt one needs to preserve continuity. One cannot think up a religion suitable to modern man out of a vacuum and then call it Christianity.

The Bible and the whole complex of initiation rites proclaim that God is very much alive, that he is the living God who has intervened in history and who still works mysteriously in history, leading mankind to its eschatological goal. Although the "God is dead" theologians bring valuable and indeed indispensable insights, some of the more extreme of them do seem to be successful in "killing" him.

Christianity, to which the believer is initiated, is essentially based on the fundamental truth that mankind was—is—in need of redemption from sin, that the son of God by his sacrificial death and glorious Resurrection achieved that redemption, and that the Church—the mystical body of the Incarnate Son—applies the fruits of that redemption to the individual as a member of a Church and through Christ offers worship to the Father.

These ideas may be strange to modern man. Psychiatry and the social sciences have tended to give him the impression that sin can be explained away. Often actions formerly looked upon as wicked are explained away by saying with understanding or contempt that the persons who did them are "sick." However, this attitude may be diminishing among experts, and this reversal of attitudes will filter down, perhaps to alter the climate of opinion. J. P. Sartre admits a humanist and consequently universal morality. O. H. Mourrer, a leading behaviourist, says that "sin" is a thoroughly respectable concept. In noting this, James P. Mackey, in an article in the *Irish Theological Quarterly,*[7] refers also to what has not been respectable in the Catholic moralist's concept of sin—its legalistic and caustic approach—and outlines the antidote, a firm stress on the personal relationship between man, the moral agent, and God.

There is quite a widespread feeling also that science has discredited the Bible so that an apologetic based on the Bible is likely to be dismissed without consideration.

There is therefore a need for pre-evangelisation before the normal instruction which precedes Christian initiation is pos-

[7] October, 1966, "The Idea of Sin in the Modern World."

sible. This pre-evangelisation must start with what modern man has and what he values. If, of course (as is the case in many circles in the United States), there is still a reverence for the word of God, obviously instruction in the Christian faith as a prelude to Christian initiation can and must build on that.[8]

But for many the Biblical approach is, in the first instance, futile; it seems unreal, and hopelessly out of date in this technological era of ours. The Bible commands respect but does not inspire conviction. Although most would believe in God, although many may perfunctorily go to church, God is not a living reality in their ordinary lives. Either they have never been baptised, or their baptism has held little meaning for them and they have lapsed into indifference or open hostility to Christianity. These two possibilities may seem to be more likely in the case of England and continental countries. Nevertheless, it was an American bishop, Bishop John Wright of Pittsburgh, who said the following:

> The Second Vatican Council is an invitation to dialogue with the post-Christian, post-Jewish, post-Islam world. . . . In a culture that has calmly heard that God is dead no one will speculate very long on Leo X's reaction to the murmurings of non-monastic monks of northwestern Europe. We must realize that our dialogue is with the world of unbelief, whether dogmatic or practical.

The problem therefore, may well be regarded as two-fold: how to get those with no religion interested to the stage where they wish to be baptised into the Christian faith, and how to give a meaningful initiation into what Christianity teaches and what Christian living means for those to whom it never had much real meaning and who have lapsed from practice. However, in order not to complicate the problem, we will consider here only the first situation (a similar approach will be of value with regard to the second): how to interest modern man in the message of Christianity—how, when he has become interested and indeed, convinced and led to an initial

---

[8] A very simple modern approach from a Biblical standpoint is provided in Avery Dulles, S.J., *Apologetics and the Biblical Christ* (London: Burns & Oates, 1963).

faith, he can be initiated into the community of the Church, which is the people of God intended for man for the twentieth century just as it was for man of the first century. In the words of Father A. Nebreda, S.J.,

> God speaks to man and invites him to respond at the level of faith. But before man can respond, he must realise that he is challenged. In order that this realisation be present the hearer must be predisposed and prepared before introducing him to God's message. Without this "pre-evangelisation" a purely kerygmatic approach will lead only to an impasse.[9]

Obviously this is such a vast and complex subject that only a few lines of approach—rather than clear-cut solutions—can be suggested, and it will not be possible to go into various controversies on the subject.

Following what has been said above, it is very important to distinguish two stages in the advance towards faith. The first stage is *anthropocentric,* i.e., it starts with man as he is in his historical and social environment and prepares him for the reception of the message of the Gospel, prepares him for kerygmatic preaching, the announcing of the Good News of Salvation. This, frankly, will involve a presentation which will include apologetics, though the personality of the "witness," of the one making the presentation, will also be all-important. The purpose of this preparation and especially of the apologetic is to attempt to remove the obstacles that exist even to a consideration of the message. We shall take a very simple example: If someone believes that religion—all religion—is superstition, it is of little use proving to him from the scriptures and from the tradition that in the early Church Christians believed that baptism washes away sins and leads the baptised into a new supra-natural life.

This type of apologetics, however, is different from the old discredited polemical apologetics which the Counter-Reformation introduced. It is apologetics for the sake of kerygma.[10] Yet in the task of preparing for the preaching of the faith, apologetics has an important role, an indispensable role.

---

[9] A. M. Nebreda, S.J., *Kerygma in Crisis* (Chicago: Loyola University Press, 1965), Introduction, p. *x.*
[10] *Ibid.,* pp. 46–49.

Father Nebreda gives a more personal and more forceful example. Discussing the question of the kerygmatic approach and its relation to apologetics and how he had found that in Europe apologetics were often looked on as out of date, he goes on:

> My most interesting experience was with another young professor in Paris. When I explained to him the problem in Japan[11] and the way we tried to solve it, he said: "Father, this is not only a problem for Japan, it is the same here. Look, Father, I must honestly say that we have gone too far in France. . . . If I tell you that more than 90 per cent of the questions I get from my students in technical schools are to be met at the apologetic level, I do not exaggerate. Now what is the use of answering an apologetically loaded question by saying, 'Wait a minute, I am going to tell you what our faith is.' That is absurd. He is asking you 'How can you explain this?' and you say, 'I do not want to discuss that, now I am going to proclaim what the mystery of Christ is.' After a while, the youngster, unimpressed, goes away." [12]

Christian faith, adds Fr Nebreda, is indeed a mystery—a mystery of God (grace) and a mystery of man (liberty). But we must not forget that the faith is also *reasonable*.

The Vatican Council's approach is anthropocentric in this sense—especially *Gaudium et Spes*. The Pastoral Constitution *The Church in the Modern World* takes man where it finds him and, without pretending to know all the answers to the grave problems which beset mankind at the present day, suggests that the Church has much to offer to the insights which modern man has and which the Church admires and that modern man needs the Church just as the Church needs modern man. In this way a dialogue is opened up, the possibility of relationship with modern man is established; it makes him open at least to consider the proclamation of the Christian message. What is applicable on a general level and without particular reference to apologetics is applicable in the case of individuals and with regard to the apologetic preparation for the Gospel.

This apologetic approach to prepare for faith is in keeping

[11] Fr Nebreda has worked in Japan for a number of years.
[12] *Ibid.*, p. 48.

with tradition; indeed, it has its roots in the New Testament.[13] The description of Christian initiation which we have given in the first part of the book shows the neophyte being brought to the Church by his guarantor for the catechumenate and for the gradual catechesis which at length led him to baptism.

But the Fathers by no means neglected the preparatory work which led to the neophyte coming in the first place. For an individual, of course, this may well have been the personal witness, example, and discussion with his friend or "guarantor." But part of the writing of the Fathers was definitely of an apologetic, "preparatory" nature. And it was positive apologetics. Beginning with Justin the Martyr, they never cease to demonstrate the superiority of Christian wisdom, to answer the attacks of adversaries. In very early Christian times Justin took the civilisation he was in and recognised the "Christian" values which were embodied in Greek culture and on which he could build a bridge to the faith. Greek philosophy he regarded as a preparation of the pagans for the Gospel, just as the Old Testament was a preparation for the Jews.

This idea of preparation and preparatory apologetics has been taken over (following the teaching of Pius XI, Pius XII, and John XIII) by the East Asian Study Week on Mission Catechetics at Bangkok in 1962, which has relevance for non-mission countries also when it states, "Positive apologetics proceeds from a true understanding and appreciation of whatever is good and acceptable in a man's culture." [14]

The preparatory approach to modern man, then, must take account of all that is good in the world of today—all that unconsciously is preparation for the Gospel message—and all that is bad, or at least of negative value in modern civilisation with regard to this preparation. These things are a point of departure for that initial act of conversion and faith which leads to the kerygma and catechesis that correspond to the catechumenate of the early Church.

[13] See, for example, St Paul's famous speech before the Council of the Areopagus (Acts 17:22–34).

[14] Quoted by Nebreda, op. cit., p. 90. See also pp. 89–94.

At first it will not be possible to isolate these elements into water-tight compartments. We "must take the man as he is and where he is," and thus make him open to the message of the Gospel and the Church.

The first thing necessary is to show modern man the possibility of the spiritual, to awaken in him a sense of God. As Bouyer says, "To rediscover God, we have to rediscover the spiritual in ourselves and the world around us." [15]

In order to do this, we must overcome not only intellectual difficulties—and these are considerable—but also the practical difficulty: the fact that modern life is so preoccupied with material things that there is little time—and apparently little need—for God and the spiritual, and that God is not so much denied as ignored, or else only perfunctorily given a place. In the worldwide technological civilisation there is a tendency to believe that God and religion belong to an age when science had not explained the causes of natural phenomena and religion explained the mysterious in terms of the divine. But now that science has explained so much and has given men power in many areas to control things which were formerly thought to be directly in the power of God or the gods, it is not possible for an intellectual to accept religion. He must deny religion in the name of reason and science and regard it as a superstition of non-intellectuals who reject reason for the mystical values of a religion accepted by faith.

It is not possible to attempt a refutation of these attitudes here. I have been content to point out that it is from this point of departure that one must begin the dialogue—the pre-evangelisation.

I have mentioned the obstacles first mainly to show the need for a pre-evangelisation; as I have said, preaching that Christ was the son of God and brought us redemption is not of much use with someone who does not believe in God, sin, or the need for redemption.

But there are many positive and good elements in modern

[15] Louis Bouyer, *Christian Initiation* (London: Burns & Oates, 1960), p. 9.

civilisation which can be built on and which can form a bridge to the conditions necessary for kerygma and initial faith.

The first part of the Constitution *The Church in the Modern World* gladly recognises these values in modern civilisation and does not claim them (as in former days) as all her own or as all due to her. Also, and this is of tremendous importance, the Church does not claim to have all the answers. This is extremely heartening for those engaged in pre-evangelisation and also for those who are being subjected to the process. Sanctity and openness to discussion are far more profitable attitudes with a view to opening a dialogue than is the pose of omniscience with a stock answer to every problem, the approach which used to be the stock-in-trade of the evangelist of former days. The Introductory Statement and the first part of *Gaudium et Spes* constitute a rich mine of material for pre-evangelisation. By its open confession of faults, by its attribution even of man's unbelief to the mistakes of the Church in society in the past, this document disarms the criticism that Christianity has never been what Christians maintain it is or should be. As George Bernard Shaw said, "The Church should not only teach humility, it should practise it." Modern man is far more inclined to admire the risk of genuine humility than the attitude of defending the indefensible in the name of religion or of pretending that the Church has never been on the losing side.

Thus *Gaudium et Spes* is anthropocentric without concealing the Christocentric character of the Church's essential message. In this remarkable document pre-evangelisation and kerygma are blended. The pre-evangelisation consists of describing man's problems: the fact that mankind is passing through a new stage of history with rapid social and cultural changes causing uneasiness and deep-seated anxiety and having their effects in the psychological, moral and religious spheres, so that men wonder if there are any truly permanent values. Conflicts of many kinds torment the modern world, so that it is seen to be "at once powerful and weak, capable of the noblest deals and the foulest."

In the face of all this, man is asking himself fundamental

questions about his own nature, about evil, about death. He recognises the worth of the mind, of truth, of wisdom. The dignity of the human person, and his need and right for true freedom have perhaps never in the whole history of the world been more greatly valued and respected as they are in the best thought of our age.

The Constitution shows in a non-polemical way what the Church has to offer to strengthen the good insights of modern times and to help to overcome the immense difficulties and dangers which beset the path of modern man.

This exposé shows the relevance of the Church—that it is not an old-fashioned institution of a by-gone age, scarred but of venerable beauty like the majestic ruins of an ancient cathedral or castle, a museum piece which may be admired, even nostalgically regretted perhaps, but of no avail. The Church is relevant because she has a message for the heart of man, whose fundamental desires and needs have not substantially changed. The document pictures mankind's possibilities in our twentieth-century world: "Before it is the path to freedom or to slavery, to progress or retreat, to brotherhood or hatred." These words are reminiscent of words written thousands of years ago in one of the first books of the Bible—Deuteronomy (30:19)—"I set before you life or death, blessing or curse. Choose life then. . . ."

The same choice has confronted man throughout human history: the message of the Church in urging the choice of life is perennially old and perennially fresh.

The answers to the questions man is asking, he himself realises, will not be given by his computers, by his robot satellites. They will not be found in space, however far his technical genius allows him to penetrate.

Man has found out that technical progress does not lead necessarily to better men or better deeds. Indeed, it may be abused by a breed of "clever devils." The lessons of two world wars, the scientific massacre of six million Jews, the inhumanities of concentration camps and of psychological torture make references to "medieval cruelty" anachronistic and effectually dispel the automatic dreams of "rosy dawn" of those who believed that progress inevitably tends upwards.

The situation of man in the modern world, then, in spite of tendencies to ignore religion, can make him receptive to a religion purified of non-essential, unacceptable concepts of a bygone era. The real Church proclaiming the real message of Christ can find a hearing, provided that the Church, without compromising its essential nature, can speak to modern man in a language he understands. The Church must courageously destroy the unnecessary assertions of the past in order to woo the present. Fundamentally, that is what the Vatican Council and the *aggiornamento* are about.

Sufficient has been said, I hope, to show the need for pre-evangelisation, and to indicate the forms it may take.

The next stage along the road to Christian initiation is the *kerygma,* or *evangelisation,* or the *presenting of the message of the Gospel* so that the individual is led to accept by personal conversion and conviction that Christ is the Lord, and that God speaks and acts in the Church through Christ. Just as the former stage was anthropocentric, so this stage is essentially *Christocentric.* Pre-evangelisation is the first stage of a genuine evangelisation.

The second stage was defined at the Bangkok conference as a dynamic heralding of the core of God's message: it corresponds to the preaching of the New Testament to the Jews or to those disposed to receive God's message; it also corresponds to the *rudimenta fidei,* the initial instruction given to catechumens in the early Church.

It is taken for granted here that conversion, which is the goal of this second stage, is the work of God and also the work of man. The work of God is the call: it is a grace, the invitation of God. The work of man is the response to this invitation, and although this itself is not achieved without grace, nevertheless man is free to say yes or no, and in this sense it is genuinely the work of man.

But these two mysterious actions need human means. God could have decided to do it in another way, but he chose to use human means. Faith comes from hearing, as St Paul says in the Epistle to the Romans, where, we have seen, the apostles preached before baptising. St Paul describes the process a little earlier in the same chapter:

If your lips confess that Jesus is Lord and if you believe in your heart that God raised Him from the dead, then you will be saved. By believing from the heart you are made righteous; by confessing with your lips you are saved. When scripture says: *Those who believe in him will have no cause for shame,* it makes no distinction between Jew and Greek: all belong to the same Lord who is rich enough, however many ask his help, *for everyone who calls on the name of the Lord will be saved.* But they will not ask His help unless they believe in Him, and they will not believe in Him unless they have heard of Him, and they will not hear of Him unless they get a preacher, and they will never have a preacher unless one is sent . . . (Romans 10:9–15).

The second stage needs to be combined with the third-stage *catechesis* so that the initial acceptance of the message may be taken a step farther and developed. The goal of this third stage is to initiate a man into Christian life and build within him a Christian personality: baptism will set the seal on these two stages, though obviously the developing of a Christian personality will go on through life. After baptism, however, it is no longer the role of the "catechist" but of the pastoral care of the Church to see to this development.

The whole basis of this approach is that faith must precede baptism, faith in the sense of a personal response to God's revelation and a personal commitment to the Christian life which has been unfolded to the candidate for baptism. This is very clearly a return to the tradition of the Church in the rites of initiation which we have studied. As we have seen, the profession of faith was solemnly made before actual baptism in the ceremony of the "giving back" of the Creed, of the Gospels and of the Pater Noster. The idea of the passive reception of baptism, the idea of the sacrament of baptism *giving* faith (though in one sense profoundly true) and the lack of stress on the personal effort and participation arose, as we have seen, from the custom of infant baptism.

The stages preceding baptism must be directed to awakening a dynamic personal response in the candidate so that his baptism is a personal encounter with Christ, not just a thing to be done so that he may become a member of the Church.

The whole idea of the catechetical renewal is to present

the message in such a way that this happens. There is not space or need to speak here at length of the catechetical renewal. It is best studied in books specifically written about it.

But briefly we may say that the heralding of the message, the kerygma, has suffered from Trent to the beginning of this century from the developments which we have already noted —the emphasis on definition, orthodoxy, polemical teaching. Even children were trained to be doughty controversialists who could refute error or defend the Church's teaching with formidable arguments learnt by rote. Often they were no mean casuists who could define the conditions for a mortal sin with the accuracy of a moral theologian and who could distinguish between the light and grave matter of, say, the seventh commandment with the acumen of a Philadelphia lawyer.

With regard to faith, Father Nebreda has summed up the one-sidedness of the Catholic approach (a reaction to the one-sided approach of some of the Reformers), in the following way.

During the Reformation the Protestants attacked faith both from the viewpoint of *content* (orthodoxy) and *profession.* As a result it became necessary to stress the outward profession that one was Catholic. It was natural for men such as Cardinal Bellarmine to stress in their catechesis on faith just these two points: faith as content and faith as profession. Had Catholics kept the other two aspects of faith along with these, all would have been well. But they forgot, practically speaking, to stress the other equally necessary elements: faith as commitment and faith as trust. Protestants had stressed these one-sidedly, and Catholic theologians and catechists went to the other extreme. Consequently, for at least two centuries (and I fear still today), faith has simply come to mean "orthodoxy."

We must not forget that man cannot nourish his spiritual life with orthodoxy alone. The aim of catechesis can never be simply to transmit correct information. Too often our emphasis in teaching is on correctness alone, with the result that sometimes we go overboard. Instead of orthodoxy we venerate *orthology,* the science of speaking correctly. We insist not only on thinking correctly but on speaking correctly! But there is more to Christianity than this. There must also, and above all, be correct practice, correct life, for faith *is* life.

For the last two centuries in catechetics this has practically been forgotten. It is remarkable that in the last thirty years we seem to have almost changed roles with Protestant theologians. Originally they so stressed the aspect of trust and commitment that we went to the other extreme and insisted one-sidedly on objectivity, correctness, orthodoxy. Today developments in Catholic theology are leading us to stress, even more forcefully than the Protestants, the personal aspect of faith.[16]

Once pre-evangelisation has taken place, the essential message of Christianity must be made known in a way to bring about the conversion of the hearer by a catechist who by his own life is a witness to the truth. It must be presented in a personal way: not as a series of abstract ideas. The neophyte must not be asked to believe in the Creation, the Incarnation, the Redemption, the Resurrection. He must have God presented to him as Someone, Someone who has been revealed to us in Christ, who had and has a plan for the salvation of mankind realised by the obedient dying of Christ on the cross, who lives after rising from the dead and ascending into heaven to intercede for us as mediator. God must be presented as a Person who, after creating us, keeps us in being and who, through love for us, desires us to share his divine, intimate life and whose friendship, freely given to us in Christ, satisfies the deepest needs of every human being.

So according to the description of evangelisation given at Bangkok:

> Once the believer has acquired a sense of God and appears spiritually ready to accept God's Message, a short resumé of salvation history is to be presented in such a way that the compelling fact of Christ as the Lord appears with striking clarity. In a technical world where man feels himself lost "in a lonely crowd," stressing such facts as God coming to us in Christ, Christ living among us as our friend and personally

[16] Nebreda, *op. cit.*, p. 43.

loving each of us, helps to awaken man to hope, and helps to evoke conversion.

As is evident from this short summary, full initiation must stress the key elements of the message: salvation history, centering on the person of Christ and insisting on the fact of Christ as Lord, emphasising the fact of Christ's continuing action in men's lives today—a modern statement of the famous *appetibilitas* (desirability) which St Augustine developed so well in his catechetical instruction.[17]

[17] Nebreda, *op. cit.*, p. 43.

CHAPTER VIII

CHRISTIAN INITIATION IN MISSIONARY COUNTRIES

So far, we have considered Christian initiation in the modern world of the technologically advanced West and of those centres of the East where this civilisation has profoundly influenced patterns of thought, such as Japan.

The situation in missionary countries is in many ways different. It is true that in some of the urban centres in those countries great numbers of people have been Westernised or affected by Western influence to such an extent that Fr Nebreda can say that a major challenge for the Church today is the growth of a worldwide technological civilisation. Perhaps he is inclined, on account of his Japanese experience, to exaggerate the speed at which this is taking place or the extent to which diverse cultures will be unified in the next twenty years so "that it will be difficult to find problems specific to a country like Japan, India or Africa." But there is obviously a lot of truth in what he says. Christian initiation at the present time will have to meet in these places at least some of the problems which we have already discussed as peculiar to Western civilisation.

But it is equally true that there are at present huge areas of the world where there is not a post-Christian or post-Islamic or post-any-other-kind of culture, but rather a culture which has not been radically changed as yet by modern progress and where people live by age-old traditions of their tribe or religious background. There are millions of people in "missionary" countries in the true sense of the word, people to whom the Gospel has never been preached.

I do not want to enter into the controversies between two schools of thought. One school, which is mainly French and Belgian,[1] regards the mission of the Church as the same throughout the world whether it is exercised in Paris or Timbuktu, Brussels or the Congo, New York or India, Melbourne or Indonesia. "Mission" is an ambiguous term, but to call a "missionary" someone who works to win back the working class of Europe to the Church seems to be going beyond the accepted meaning of the word and to be hardly justified from a common-sense or theological point of view. By "missionary country" I mean[2] a country where the Gospel has not been preached, or has not been accepted to such an extent that the Church is known to the vast majority of its peoples, and where the Church is not firmly implanted with an indigenous hierarchy and an adequate number of priests and bishops.

In such countries the problems and challenges of making Christian initiation meaningful are different from those in a post-Christian milieu.

It is here that the greatest possibilities exist for a real adaptation of the rites of initiation, and it is here that the greatest opportunities have been missed in the past.

The Vatican Council is very clear on the need for such adaptation, and it gives guidelines for the general approach of the Christian missionary which, of course, can and must be made to have special application to the rites of initiation:

> The seed which is the Word of God sprouts from the good ground watered by divine dew. From this ground the seed draws nourishing elements which it transforms and assimilates into itself. Finally it bears much fruit. Thus, in imitation of the plan of the Incarnation, the young Churches, rooted in Christ and built up on the foundation of the apostles, take to themselves in a wonderful exchange all the riches of the nations which were given to Christ as an inheritance (cf. Ps. 2:8). From the customs and traditions of their people, from their wisdom and their learning, from their arts and sciences, these

---

[1] See especially A. M. Henry, O.P., *A Mission Theology* (Notre Dame, Ind.: Fides, 1962).

[2] Following Eugene Hillman, C.S.Sp., *The Church as Mission* (New York: Herder & Herder, 1965).

Churches borrow all those things which can contribute to the glory of their Creator, the revelation of the Saviour's grace, or the proper arrangement of Christian life.

If this goal is to be achieved, theological investigation must necessarily be stirred up in each major socio-cultural area, as it is called. In this way, under the light of the tradition of the universal Church, a fresh scrutiny will be brought to bear on the deeds and words which God has made known, which have been consigned to sacred Scripture, and which have been unfolded by the Church Fathers and the teaching authority of the Church.

Thus it will be more clearly seen in what ways faith can seek for understanding in the philosophy and wisdom of these peoples. A better view will be gained of how their customs, outlook on life, and social order can be reconciled with the manner of living taught by divine revelation. As a result, avenues will be opened for a more profound adaptation in the whole area of Christian life. Thanks to such a procedure, every appearance of syncretism and of false particularism can be excluded, and Christian life can be accommodated to the genius and the dispositions of each culture.

Particular traditions, together with the individual patrimony of each family of nations, can be illumined by the light of the gospel, and then be taken up into Catholic unity. Finally, the individual young Churches, adorned with their own traditions, will have their own place in the ecclesiastical communion, without prejudice to the primacy of Peter's See, which presides over the entire assembly of charity.

And so, it is to be hoped and is altogether fitting that Episcopal Conferences within the limits of each major socio-cultural territory will be so united among themselves that they will be able to pursue this program of adaptation with one mind and with a common plan.[3]

The Liturgy Constitution, in the section headed *Norms for the Adaptation of the Liturgy to the Genius and Traditions of Peoples,* states that the Church has no wish to impose a conformity in matters which do not involve the faith or the good of the whole community. Rather she respects and fosters the spiritual adornments and gifts of the various races and peoples. Anything in their way of life that is not indissolubly bound up with superstition and error she studies with

[3] Decree on the Church's Missionary Activity, *The Documents of Vatican II* Nos. 22, 23, pp. 612–13.

sympathy and, if possible, preserves intact. Sometimes, in fact, she admits such things into the liturgy itself, as long as they harmonize with its true and authentic spirit.

Provided that the substantial unity of the Roman rite is maintained, the revision of liturgical books should allow for legitimate variations and adaptations to different groups, religions and peoples, especially in mission lands. Where opportune, the same rule applies to the structuring of rites and the devising of rubrics.

Within the limits set by the typical editions of the liturgical books, the constitution lays down that it shall be for the competent territorial ecclesiastical authority mentioned in No. 22, par. 2, to specify adaptations, especially in the case of the administration of the sacraments, the sacramentals, processions, liturgical language, sacred music, and the arts; but this must still be done according to the fundamental norms laid down in this Constitution.

The Constitution goes on:

> In some places and circumstances, however, an even more radical adaptation of the liturgy is needed and entails greater difficulties.
> Therefore:
> (1) The competent territorial ecclesiastical authority mentioned in Article 22, § 2, must, in this matter, carefully and prudently consider which elements from the traditions and genius of individual peoples might appropriately be admitted into divine worship. Adaptations which are judged to be useful or necessary should then be submitted to the Apostolic See, by whose consent they may be introduced.
> (2) To ensure that adaptations are made with all necessary circumspection, the Apostolic See will grant power to this same territorial ecclesiastical authority to permit and to direct, as the case requires, the necessary preliminary experiments over a determined period of time among certain groups suited for the purpose.
> (3) Because liturgical laws often involve special difficulties with respect to adaptation, particularly in mission lands, men who are experts in these matters must be employed to formulate them.[4]

[4] Liturgy Constitution, Nos. 37–41, in *The Documents of Vatican II*, pp. 151–152.

This section marks a great advance in thinking and practice with regard to missionary lands and people living in them. It definitely rejects the old ideas of a kind of spiritual colonialism whereby the Western Church exported not only the teaching of the Church and rites essential to her liturgy, but also the Western customs of certain stages of Western civilisation, as part of them. A new era is ushered in full of significance for local churches in missionary lands and for the missionaries who go to serve them.

Although in recent years more latitude for adaptation had been given even before the Council and enlightened missionary thinkers had championed the idea of diversity of practice within unity of worship, the importance of the above solemn statements is that this new attitude is now the official mind of the Church, and the way is open to extend the pioneering work of adaption done in scattered parts of the world to the whole of the Church in the mission lands.

We have said already that most religions have initiation rites. The ancient Greeks, the Romans, the Jews of the centuries about the time of Christ, the ancient Egyptians—all had their initiation rites which have some ideas similar to the ideas expressed in Christian initiation. Similarly, in our day, Hindus and Moslems have elaborate rites of initiation and the primitive religions of Africa and the East also have theirs.[5] There is a wide variety, of course, with regard to the modes of initiation and the different types of ritual, which it would not be possible even to mention here.

But patient research and thorough acquaintance with such religious initiation rites and their deep and often hidden meaning can reveal many sterling elements on which Christian initiation might build. The ceremonies of baptism and confirmation and the eucharist might thereby become more meaningful to indigenous and could be seen as a perfection of tribal and other religious rites rather than as a complete break with the past and the adopting of imported religious experience.

The Liturgy Constitution is an invitation to separate the elements which need to be changed or abandoned in present-

[5] See C. J. Bleeker, ed., *Initiation* (Leiden: E. J. Brill, 1965), p. 15.

day pagan ceremonies and in the rites of religions such as the Moslem and the Hindu. This has been attempted in some parts of the world, and since the Council great impetus has been given to such movements.

It must be stressed, of course, that it is for local experts and local hierarchies to decide about particular customs which could be Christianized and even taken up in the Christian liturgy. It must be emphasised, too, that work in this field has not been going on for long or in many places, but it is hoped that after the Council more research and experimentation may take place along the lines which pioneers have already mapped out.

One example from the Congo may be used to illustrate what a wealth of material awaits the Christian liturgist in indigenous initiation rites. Part of the interest and value of this illustration lies in the fact that the description of it comes from a Congolese priest who draws from his personal knowledge and experience as well as from the researches of European and African colleagues. This African priest, Father Celestin Mubengayi Lwakale, C.I.C.M., has published his work in this field, as a thesis for his degree in the Gregorian University in Rome, and a version has been published in French in Leopoldville in the Congo.[6]

After chapters on the sacramentals and the sacramental system of the Church and the relationship of African culture towards them, the author has a section describing possibilities of adaptation and transition from cultural traditions of Africa and especially the Congo to Christian ritual. He states his conclusion first:

It is possible by means of conscientious study to discover in African rites and symbols a religious base which can be sublimated by divine grace. Even in their superstitious (not to say immoral) aspects, these rites always tend towards giving life its religious orientation, its full value and conformity to the law which the Supreme Being has given to us through our ancestors: whether there is a question of individual or collective offerings, engagement and marriage ceremonies, of birth

[6] *The Christian Sacramental System and Christianization in Depth* (Rome and Leopoldville, 1966).

and naming, the rites of initiation or the ritual connected with widowhood.[7]

This conclusion is based on the beautiful analysis which he gives of the traditional rites of his people. While recognising their imperfections, he shows how in the past they have been misunderstood by moralists. The religious practices of Africans and of the Bantu, and particularly those of the Congo, are not "magic" in the true sense of the word— as they have often been believed to be by Western missionaries, for example, in the sense of Father Haring's definition of magic as "a turning away from God and a turning towards impersonal forces, even to the enemy of God: it is false worship, the opposite of worship." Father Lwakale sees various ritual manifestations on the part of Africans not as "magical" in this way but rather as an attempt at a liturgy of cosmic religion which should find its fulfilment in Christian liturgy. The various fetishes and amulets that pagan Africans have recourse to are related to the Supreme Being by the prayers which make them sacred. For example, there is the amulet which a sterile woman wears in order to become fertile. This is blessed by a rite by which the woman places herself under the protection of God and prays for children to God, who knows the secrets of nature. The rite includes a touching passage: "O God, Father of all wisdom, who knows both day and night. Why are you hostile to me? All my friends have wives who have children. I am unfortunate. Why?" This is a prayer of a Maluba from the Katanga region of the Congo.

There are many other "blessed" charms and amulets which enter into the daily life of the Bantu. Missionaries have often given them the generic name of "ju-ju" and regarded them as evil; but they cannot be classed as "magic" in the bad sense of the word. Their inner meaning prevents such a classification.

These objects cannot be understood except from a vital and fundamentally existential point of view: they must be seen in a setting of cosmology summarised thus: GOD, NA-

[7] *Ibid.*, p. 53.

TURE, MAN, HAPPINESS. God is the Creator. Only in him is
the equation Wisdom—Love—Life realised. Apparently the
Creator has left the work of creation unfinished so that in
making use of it man can at one and the same time discover
God's power and man's weakness. God has, however, left
some of his power in nature. And so Africans try to get for
themselves this force which things possess. Hence the use of
objects such as leopard's teeth and leopard's skin and so on.

The beautiful prayers that they say in practising their ritual
prove that the Bantus do not wish to act against the will of
God. They do not even think of doing it, still less of wanting
to do it. Their ritual practices, improperly called "magical"
according to Father Lwakale, are the prayers of men at the
mercy of a Nature which is harsh, but of which modern man
has discovered some of the laws.

Father Lwakale admits that in some of the rites there may
be an element of magic, even "black magic" when evil people try to use the rites for evil ends. But he rightly maintains
that there are so many beautiful Bantu ceremonies and
prayers that could easily be adapted by the Church and that
would be more meaningful than the blessings and ceremonies
as they are now in the Roman Ritual.

The traditional rites of Africa are imperfect because they
do not bear witness explicitly to faith in Christ: pagan
"priests" expect the effects they desire to happen automatically—*ex opere operato*—whereas by the sacramentals of
the Church, Christians express their obedience and faith in
God, base their expectations on the merits of Christ and revive the sense of their conversion and their adherence to God
by the liturgy. This is the difference between the sacramentals
of the Church and traditional African rites. This is why the
Church in her prayer could absorb pagan rites without prejudice, clothe them with true Christian meaning, assess their
relationship to African religious culture in order to integrate
them if possible into the liturgy. Here there is the problem
of adaptation of worship, or rather the direction which this
adaptation should take. Incidentally, Father Lwakale denies
that any African rites can in any sense be regarded as devil
worship either explicitly or implicitly. As he says: "The most

pagan of pagans would never think of having anything to do with the devil, the personal enemy of God whom none can resist and before whom all creatures are powerless." [8]

All this is not of direct concern, but it is useful, especially for those not acquainted with the potential riches of the African spiritual heritage, and will serve as an introduction to the treatment of our specific subject: a study of rites of African initiation to show that it has some of the characteristics of Christian initiation and that it could therefore be utilised in adapting Christian initiation rights in an African setting. And what applies to Africa and the Congo may well be regarded as a model (with necessary modifications according to circumstances) of other pagan rites and rites of non-Christian religions in other parts of the world.

The African rites of initiation of which we are speaking here are not the initiation into a secret society, a sort of magic sect; it has its secrets, of course, and they are communicated to those who are initiated so that they can make the passage to adulthood. Initiation, as it is understood here, is a rite of passage from one state to another, from one age group to another. This initiation goes on throughout life right up to the moment of death.

Indeed, in certain regions of the Congo, the life of a child is, so to speak, entirely a ritual initiation (especially among the Lulua and the Baluba of Kasai). The very first "rite of passage" is the "coming out," the solemn presentation of the child about a week after his birth. A "priest," the mother of the family or the uncle on the mother's side, performs the rite, presenting the baby to the sun, the symbol of God, with words of blessing pronounced in the name of the community or the clan which greets its new member.

This ritual ceremony is common to the whole of black Africa, in spite of the differences in the manner of performing it, and whether it is called "the ceremony of the eighth day" or any other title. The solemn "coming out" of the newly born child is the rite which has for its purpose the consecration of the child to the Creator, even if at times the folklore aspects of the feast conceal the religious aspirations which are awakened and contained in the rite.

It is the same in many provinces of the Congo and in other African countries, where the "first right of passage" of man, his entry into the community, is characterised by the ceremony of "coming out" and the giving of a name, without initiation being necessarily mentioned. A further step is marked by the first cutting of the hair among the Lulua and the Baluba. Here again symbolism plays a role. Every act which somehow implies an eternal lessening must be accompanied by a progressive consciousness of the personality, and a sacred, a liturgical or ritual atmosphere is necessary for it. Mixed up among many vain observances, even superstitions, this atmosphere continues throughout the African child's development, at its first cutting of teeth, the physiological manifestations of puberty, right up to the solemn and spectacular moment, after the long moral and civic formation, of the great rite of initiation which consecrates the definitive entry into the community.

Another important point is that the rite of traditional initiation in Africa does not necessarily involve circumcision as such. Actually, in many countries this operation does coincide with the time of initiation, but it is not practised throughout the whole of Africa. In the Congo, for example, it no longer exists in certain provinces or it exists in a very simplified and modified form.

Nevertheless, it is in the traditional circumcision that we find the spiritual meaning of initiation. If such meaning is present, one can Christianize this rite without undue uniformity and without rejecting the real values which Christian teaching can use.

Father Graverand, quoted by Father Lwakale, has suggested three stages of adaptation. First of all the stage of "breaking away" should proclaim the transcendence of the Christian message over the "mysteries" of the pagan so as to avoid every equivocal compromise with pagan customs which are superstitions or immoral. The next stage is that of "interpretation," and this helps Africans to see the values which these rites possess and the limit beyond which they

were not able to go. The third stage, that of "cultural adaptation," consists of integrating into Christianity the pagan rites
which have been carefully purified from their unsuitable local
accretions. The Christianization of the rites of initiation consists in a use of those teachings of initiation rites which can
find their fulfilment in Christian mystery—such as the initiation themes of death and life. Such adaptation will be a real
progress to fulfilment in Christ.

THE RITES OF ADOLESCENT INITIATION

The family takes this rite very seriously and takes part in
it, and the tribal community itself has a prominent role. In
some tribes, circumcision takes place at the age of five years
but in others it is part of the initiation ceremonies of adolescence and it is the latter we will be concerned with.

The circumcision is a way of progressing towards a new
life; a period of training and formation is organised for the
group who are to be circumcised and initiated. During this
time, in the village their mothers say prayers and sing religious chants.

The boys are sent to a camp situated some distance from
the village for a period of three to six weeks (depending on
the region in which they live). The young men go there with
an affected air of cheerfulness, encouraging each other at
intervals because they know that what they are going to do
is dangerous; but the fear of danger is wiped out by the hope
of getting their new name, which will guarantee their title
of true member of the tribe. This formation has been compared to a novitiate because of the community life of the
youths, who will be adults when they come out of this seclusion. What sort of a formation is given in the camp of initiation? Some have thought that it was a type of military service.
This is not completely inaccurate. Civic formation, however,
plays its part and is not least in importance. The idea is to
inspire the young men with a love of the community and a
respect for their own person which is precious in the eyes of
God and of men. To reply to this question completely it
would be necessary to study ethnology, which would take us

too far; all we have in mind at present is a modest catechetical and theological study.

The period preceding the young men's circumcision is com-
parable to a retreat. They submit to a very severe programme: a time of prolonged silence, a time of recreation
and relaxation, a time of physical exercise. A number of
taboos are placed on them with a view to personal discipline,
because the community must have men of character and
strong will. That is why they are served with food which is
ill prepared. They sleep on the ground with scanty clothing
and very little protection against cold and storms. Why? Because in order to become a man it is necessary to overcome
oneself, to overcome one's body, to overcome natural in-
clinations. It is necessary to merit a new name. They are
told that they have retired from the world to enter it again
as "new men" at the end of the period in the camp. The
community expects them to be men of character and strong
will, capable of defending the tribe even at the cost of their
life.

Can one say that a moral education is given to young
Africans during the period of initiation? A civic morality is
certainly taught, involving obedience to tribal authority and
to the authority of their fathers. A collection of customs such
as that made by Henri Junod in his book *Moeurs et coutûmes
des Bantous* show how imperfect is the teaching given at the
camp; but this imperfection could be a preparation for a
more perfect catechesis of the real Christian truth which
alone is capable of expanding the fundamental aspirations of
these young men. Some of the moral formation which is given
at these camps is really trivial. The only interest which this
teaching offers to African theologians is that it is an approach
—albeit a halting one—to the true life. Although it is not possible to look here for stones with which to build Christianity,
the imperfections which are hidden in pagan religions nevertheless show their aspirations to that elevation which will be
given them by Christianity. And we should note that the
formation has a quality which interests Africans very much:
"life as a vital personal force and as a dynamism shared with
all the members of the clan." In this formation also there is

an attempt to teach certain notions of the transmission of life, but this is done very clumsily even in the delicate domain of sexuality. By certain stereotyped formulae the head of the camp keeps the traditional wisdom which invites the young men to exalt their virility and its privileges, their paternity, and ideas of the domination over the female, who is regarded as something apart, put on the lowest moral or religious level. (However, Bantu wisdom does give a special place to the mother. There are many beautiful stories and fables which teach filial piety as the response to the love of an African mother.)

If the rite of initiation includes circumcision, the operation takes place in the camps of initiation and the cuts are taken care of on the spot. The rest of the programme of the camps consists in preparing for the return of the young men to normal life as "new men" conscious of their future responsibilities. During this time they are formed for their future role as men by combats and by flogging of each other. The Bambara practise ritual suffering which will lead them to symbolic death and to a share in the divine nature. By the imposing of a secret they become accustomed to silence, to the control of their tongue and the control of themselves. By the accomplishment of the grave and solemn rites such as sacrifices and the revealing of the mysteries of the brotherhood, they acquire spiritual maturity and a sense of their responsibilities. This self-knowledge is accompanied by a vital need for union with the Godhead. Those to be initiated receive indoctrination which increases the religious signification of the rite of initiation: "Each morning and each evening they greet the sun, the symbol of God. In the morning they reply to the chants of their mothers who are singing in the village."

THE END AND THE RETURN

The end of the camp coincides with the complete healing of the wounds of circumcision. It marks also the end of their state as children and the commencement of a new dimension as men who henceforth will participate with full right in the social life of the tribe. Formation of the camp follows an excellent teaching procedure which teaches the maturing of the personality as a continuity which recalls the old way of life and suggests the new life which is to come. This is shown by a Pigmy chant of initiation:

> You are no longer a son of the night which is dark and treacherous, which is black as the soot of your smoke-filled house. You are not the son of the night, you are the son of the brilliant and clear day, the son of the earth which is red and generous, the earth which brings forth tasteful fruit. You are the sons of the day which is brilliant and clear, no, you are not the sons of the night.

In the Cameroon among the Beti, nine burdens, or the nine obligations imposed by the Creator, are sung at this time. "God has given nine burdens, it is the law. Who neglects even one of them, has committed a sin." Then it goes on to give the nine commandments which contain in an imperfect way some of the Ten Commandments, especially with regard to killing, stealing, giving false witness, and adultery. This traditional morality, which is inculcated at their entrance into a new phase of human life, will naturally find its perfecting in the teaching of the Bible. The Bible also speaks of the new condition of the baptized pagan who has to abandon his own way of life to lead a new life in Christ. "I want to urge you in the name of the Lord not to go on living the aimless kind of life that pagans live. Intellectually they are in the dark, and they are estranged from the life of God, without knowledge because they have shut their hearts to it (Ephesians 4:17–18)." Chapter 5 of Ephesians, which constitutes truly the moral code of those initiated into the mystery of Christianity, of those who must behave like leaven in the mass, is also worthy of study and comparison.

Before those who have been initiated leave, they destroy the camp, and then they take a bath. After having passed several weeks in a state of corporal penance, they throw into the river the old clothes which they have worn up to now. Clothed in the most beautiful clothes, they are triumphantly welcomed in the village. The heads of the camp are given payment for their work and the feast continues in the jubilation exactly as today we acclaim the neophytes or newly confirmed—with this difference: that baptism and confirmation are primarily a fulfilment in the sacrifice of the Mass, while the ceremonies of initiation generally close with a communal family repast offered in honour of the ancestors. In some tribes a hymn of thanksgiving and of propitiation is addressed to the ancestors, the founders of the tribe and of the rites. The comparison with Christian rites of initiation is clear.

THE MEANING AND SPIRITUAL SIGNIFICATION OF THE RITE OF INITIATION

The rites of initiation have three main elements: the consecration of life, the entry or incorporation into the community, and the giving of a new name.

Father Lwakale relates that he found a very curious and astonishing fact. When his fellow countrymen were asked about the meaning of the rite of initiation, especially accompanied by circumcision, all replied: "It is a baptism." Indeed, traditional initiation is a consecration, an offering of one's life to the Creator by the community. This meaning of consecration of the person to God is clear when one realises that the complete rite implies a shedding of blood, which points to the intention of sacrifice and offering; the isolation stresses this spiritual and traditional meaning of the rite as does the discipline imposed on those initiated and on the tribal community during the time of preparation. But in this consecration of life, the amin idea is that of death followed by a resurrection symbolised in this way: death to childhood, awakening (or resurrection) to the state of being an adult. This agrees to an astonishing degree with the meaning which St Paul gives to baptism—first of all death to our previous life, which is buried with the dead Christ, and then a rebirth (therefore a resurrection) to a new life that one shares with the risen Christ.

During the time of their formation those to be initiated mime death and resurrection. Unwittingly, they are acting out the mystery of spiritual fruitfulness prophesied by Jesus.

The ceremony symbolises this death and "resurrection" to a new life as follows:

The one who is to be initiated lies prostrate on the ground in the camp. The chief says to him "You are dead?", and he replies "I am dead." Then the chief asks him if he wants to come to life again and be able to eat and drink or if he wants to remain dead. When the one to be initiated says he wants to live, the chief tells him to be strong and always to keep his head high, to keep the path of righteousness and never to flee in the face of difficulties. It was for this that he acted out death and victory over self.

Entry into the Community

The right of initiation is also the juridical and solemn entry of the candidate into the community as a full-grown man, an adult. The tribal chief himself receives the new members and makes the official declaration that they were adults. This declaration means that they must be given a new name.

Giving of a new Name

Following the rite of initiation, a new name is given to each successful candidate. In the mind of Africans, the name is one with the person. Those who have undergone the rites of initiation have by this very fact changed their personality; it is to be expected therefore that a new name would be given as a perpetual reminder of this.

Father O. Dufonten sums up the meaning of initiation thus:

In the African mentality initiation, of which circumcision is one of the principal rites, strengthens the personal life of the Nsundi, intensifies his belonging to the tribe, makes more serious the guilt of those who after their initiation transgress the laws of the tribe. The giving of a new name is a sign of this strengthening of life. Initiation is so important that a woman will absolutely refuse to have marital relations with her husband who has not been circumcised.[9]

[9] Quoted by C. M. Lwakale, *op. cit.*, pp. 68–69.

CHRISTIANIZATION OF THE RITE
OF INITIATION

According to the general principles with regard to adaptation, it permits native rites and customs and transcendent religion such as Christianity to join forces with the existential condition of a man, and it throws into greater relief the immanent character of the religion of Christ. There are a number of examples of how this could be done. On the eighth day of the rite we have discussed, there are religious rites such as the official coming out of the child and his presentation to the sun, and on the same day there is the giving of a name to the newborn baby. There would be value, it seems, in combining these rites with the ceremonies of baptism in order to realise the desire of Africans to consecrate their children to God. These two initiations, that of the tribe and that of baptism, could be made to coincide. Taboos imposed on those to be initiated and also on the community are an ascetical discipline. The teaching of Christian ascetism, which seeks, through our own painful efforts, to make us conform internally to Christ, could give a great spiritual support to these taboos. It would be necessary to train some of the people who carry out the traditional initiation so that they could place the traditional rites in a new context without loss.

It would be worthwhile where possible to have the rite of initiation occur during the catechumenate of adults. A number of these rites prepare the understanding for the moment of initiation. The seclusion of the initiated could be easily understood within the framework of a preparatory retreat for baptism. It would also indicate the need for a mystical death. If a new Christian catechesis took points of departure in African tradition, it would not begin from man himself or from the universe but from the very mystery of the living God who has spoken and who calls us from Satan.

We have already mentioned the importance of the name which is given to those being initiated. By means of this name they acquire a full consciousness of their special responsibility. It is worthwhile to give value to this name at baptism, either by adopting this as a baptismal name or at least by including it. In fact, Father Lwakale suggests that the tribal name could well be given instead of a saint's name because the tribal names are chosen by the parents to refer to the heroic ancestors of the clan, who had a special relationship to God.

TRADITIONAL INITIATION—A SACRAMENT OF CONFIRMATION

Could the traditional initiation be made a sacramental of the sacrament of confirmation? Before replying to this question, we must consider two points. First of all, the sacramentals play an essentially functional role with regard to the sacraments. Adapted as they are to the existential conditions of a man of flesh and blood, they strike our imagination, speak to the intelligence through the medium of the senses and touch our hearts more easily to the great profit of the moral efficacy of the sacraments. The episcopate of the Congo expressed this desire:

> It seems necessary in general and all things being duly considered to adapt the rites of the sacraments and sacramentals to local customs. In the first place, to suppress the rites and texts which are out of accord with the local mentality. The rites of traditional initiation could therefore be celebrated in a Christian fashion as a kind of para-liturgy and could accompany the administration of baptism or be inserted into the period of their catechumenate. It also seems to us that this christianized rite could be wonderfully adapted to the meaning and spirit of confirmation. More and more the solemn profession of faith coincides with that of confirmation. It has become common in the Congo and in the whole of Africa. It is the ideal moment for pastoral work to accept the contribution of the spirit of the initiation ceremony and not its letter only.

It would be necessary to take from the rite certain old and incompatible usages which do not suit the present African development, to keep the spirit of strictness and asceticism and its ability to awaken a sense of responsibility, and to allow it in this way to correspond to the needs of the young

Christian who wishes to be a soldier in the cause of Christ.

For Africans who have been converted, initiation is still an essential step in their way through life; the passage from infancy to puberty and from puberty to the adult state demands a rite of a religious and communal character. For young men and also for girls, it is a question of becoming conscious of their vocation in all its dimensions, to face life as a mission. And so the chants, songs and dances which accompany or follow the rites of initiation stress this mission with a striking reality. The words call to mind the mystery of life, the actions symbolize the transmission of life so clearly that the attitudes of the initiated and of the audience sometimes offend against modesty.

To be initiated into life in order to consecrate it, to consecrate life in order to introduce a man juridically into the community—that is the fundamental sacred meaning of the rite of initiation. It was wrong for the first missionaries to see the rites of initiation only as ceremonies to be reprobated, purely erotic procedures filled with immorality and sensuality. These aspects, which are not altogether absent, do not come into the rite in order to express the fundamental content of it, the mystery of fecundity as such, which is consecrated to God, to the creation of life and to the protecting spirits. This mystical meaning is expressed by means of sacrifice, by an offering of the person, an offering made sometimes with realism by blood, by circumcision, or in certain cases by infliction of tribal markings. This shows that there is a philosophy in these rites which should be brought to light.

INITIATION AND SACRAMENTAL PROCEDURES

The rite of initiation is of great interest for catechesis in Africa, at least in those places where Africans still attach importance to the ceremony of initiation. We add this restriction because before formulating practical suggestions we must take account of the cultural development of African society and the importance which the rite has at the present time. But it is necessary to realise that even when the rite itself has disappeared gradually, the mystical meaning which gave it a living meaning persists. The practice of adaptation must not merely have recourse to a custom considered from the material point of view—but rather to the spirit of it, in order to profit by this mystical element "of expansion of the personality by an effective participation in the life of the community." These realities, however small their spiritual content, lie hidden within the rites and customs of Africa even though these are imperfect, but they are only fully realised in the perfect form which they prepared for: the law of grace. And so it is in the true sacraments of Christian initiation that the relationship between them and the rites of traditional initiation is most clearly seen: baptism and confirmation. Christian initiation and traditional initiation are different, but they complement each other in the sense that the first was prepared for by the second. It is true that the rite of initiation and all the rites which prepared a welcome for the Redemption of Christ are spiritually ineffective. They inculcate and give a national consciousness of responsibility within a restricted community, whereas the rite of Christian initiation is an efficacious symbol which gives the grace it speaks about. The sacrament of confirmation, which perfects our configuration of Christ, gives to the one confirmed the Holy Spirit, source of the indispensable social virtues which the Christian must practise to live up to his vocation. By the African rite of initiation the chief of the tribe solemnly introduces the individual into the community. This recalls to him the role played by the bishop in the rite of confirmation. The chief of the diocese—the bishop—actually receives solemnly those which baptism has made juridically members of the mystical body of Christ and reminds them of the obligations which, while they were still little children, they accepted in baptism.

The traditional rite of initiation does not produce the effects which are contained inherently in it and also in the form of the ceremonies. The rite of confirmation, on the other hand, gives a communication of the Holy Spirit and produces in our soul the basis of all Christian activity in the world: love.

The spirit of attachment and fidelity which Africans have

towards their tribe, and which they express towards it, could extend to Christ and to His kingdom, conceived of as the great tribe of the descendants of Christ. Once again, it is not a question of establishing an identity between sacraments and traditional rites but of considering the traditional rites as signs capable of becoming Christian sacramentals, to the great profit of the sacraments themselves. In the composition of an African ritual and of the catechism there is an opportunity for an authentic Christianization of the rite of initiation. This should not keep blindly to the letter, which today is limited in many ways, but should carefully guard the spirit of it. The actors, so to speak, will remain the same, but the scene will change: it will become the scene of the true worship, formerly prefigured by the communal family meal which is a figure of the Eucharistic sacrifice and communion. The tribal family would be the "mission" or the "parish," the leader of the tribe is now the bishop, the parishioners are members of the living community in the midst of which the confirmed will exercise their rites and accomplish their duties.

However, an example from the East—initiation rites in Java—shows a more unpromising situation than that we have just considered. Nevertheless it may have elements which could be utilised.[10]

Initiation practices in Java can be found among the people who are in possession of esoteric doctrines called *ngelmu kasampurnam,* or doctrine of profession. Generally speaking, the *ngelmu* is a more or less secret Javanese science handed down by *ngelmu guru,* or experts. A very important part of this Javanese science is the doctrine of perfection which tells of God, creation, eternity, etc., and teaches the way for man to return to God. These ideas are traditions stemming from the heathen and Hindu times which later on underwent some alterations under the influence of Islam. Most of these traditions have been collected in the holy book, the *Serat Wirid.* The doctrine in the *Wirid* is given in metaphor, mystery and paradox. When the Javanese occupies himself with questions of the end of man and his relation to God he likes to do this

[10] Dr Th. Tangelder, M.Sc., *Sacramenten en Volksgebruiken* (Bussum: Paul Brand, N.U., 1950).

metaphorically. There must be a shroud of mystery around it. The book itself, which is full of riddles and mysterious phrases, is meant for the teachers of the doctrine only. In order to become a pupil, one must bind oneself to one teacher and promise not to visit other teachers, and to initiate no one else in the doctrine unless such a person is dying. In order to increase the air of mystery, the *guru*—the teacher —gives only private lessons; the pupil visits him at stated hours to pass on a few words of wisdom at a time. The teacher whispers some lines into his pupil's ear, for example: "Look for the life that gives life," or "The youngest is older than the oldest," or "The earth is buried in the ground," etc. The pupil is then left for some minutes of meditation and after a while the *guru* repeats the mysterious lines. At the end of the session the teacher says: "If you understand this, hide it in your heart; if you do not understand, be content but go on seeking until you find."

Now we come to the actual ritual of initiation. The initiation takes place on a certain date in the middle of the night. The teacher and his pupil follow the narrow jungle path up the mountain to a place far removed from the village that has been chosen for the initiation. At a lonely spot some older pupils are waiting patiently for the *guru* and his disciple. A small distance away is a small pond, the source of the mountain stream. A few mats are spread out and are covered with seven white cotton cloths; on top scented flowers, the *kenanga* flowers, are strewn. This is the place of initiation.

In the meantime the *guru* and his disciple have gone to the water while they pray: "I am looking for holy water in order to wash my small and big uncleanliness away because of God, the Very High."

After returning from the water, three sacrifices are prepared. The first is destined to be offered to the great Prophet. The second is offered to the ancestors, and the third is a sacrifice of praise to one of the *Walis,* the traditional Islam teachers.

Meanwhile, one of the pupils has taken off the top part of his clothing. On his head he carries a *kuluk* or ceremonial cap. Round the neck are chains of flowers, and flowers also hang from his ears. In this way he is dressed like the subject of the sultan who goes to visit his lord. This same initiation will lead him as a subject into the spiritual realm of the unseen and the One on high.

The pupil kneels down and one of the witnesses throws incense on the fire. This implores God's blessing on the initiation. Then the teacher kneels down beside the pupil and whispers holy teaching into his ear. This teaching usually deals with the relation of God to man and vice versa and often is coloured with pantheism.

After the ceremony there is a sacrificial meal, after which everything that is left can be taken home as a sign of blessing. The pupil has now been given a share in the wisdom of life of his forefathers and has been initiated in the mysteries of life surrounding him. In the stillness of the night he feels closer to the unseen maker of the universe. The form in which the ceremony takes place depends largely on the local initiative and intelligence of the *guru*.

The first question to be asked from the point of view of adaptation is if these initiation rites are linked up with religious error and if this link is unbreakable. In order to find the answer we must distinguish between the content and the form of the initiation. It seems that the content is inseparably linked with religious error. The idea of God which is basic to it shows too strongly the heterogenous influences which have worked on it. In some areas which are more closely linked with Islam, we find the monotheistic idea, one God really different from all the rest of creation. In places more closely linked with the real Javanistic tradition we find very often a pantheistic view of life. Therefore, because the idea of God is rather vague and uncertain and because of the remarkable mixture of different errors in the *ngelmu,* the holy book, a direct adaptation with regard to the content seems to be excluded.

The *form* in which these initiations take place is a different matter. To this belong the metaphor, the symbol, the wise sayings, the language of riddles, the whole motley cloak of mystery in which these utterings are shrouded and which give to it a special attraction. This air of mystery explains why the sayings are given to the pupils bit by bit and also why proclamation is avoided. To preserve the same air of mystery, the initiation takes place at a lonely spot where not everybody can go, and only witnesses who are already initiated are allowed to be there.

These forms now used for the communication of error could be used for communication of true doctrines; and these forms are so valuable that it seems highly desirable and warranted to retain them. The particular rites and practices in which an initiation actually takes place are so varied that their value is not very great for adaptation purposes, but the general forms of the initiation which we have described above and which are binding on all the *ngelmus* represent values which are worthy of retention by Christianity. This general form of initiation seems to us very valuable because it shows a great reverence and respect for the mystery. There is not here space to include more examples of possibilities of adaptation. Moreover, as we have indicated, many of these are in an embryonic state and have only been published in provisional form, if at all. A very useful service, nevertheless, would be served by collecting all the efforts at adaptation that are being made.

The developments which have taken place in the ideas of the catechetics and liturgy in recent years have been written up generally in the form of symposia containing the papers of conferences. Some noteworthy ones will be mentioned here because they are having and will have a decisive effect on Christian initiation with regard to all four classes of adults and children to which we have already referred.

The International Study Week on *Mission and Liturgy* at Nijmegen, Holland from 12th to 19th September, 1959, was an outgrowth of the "International Congress on Pastoral Liturgy" held at Assisi and Rome in 1956.

The object of the meeting was clear to the organisers from the very first discussions: the Study Week should concentrate upon the particular missionary value of well-formed worship. The study meeting of missionaries at Assisi had confirmed once again what mission experts had emphasised over and over again in the past, namely, that those engaged in mission work have paid too little attention to the proper formation of Christian worship. They must, therefore, be made acutely aware of the missionary value of the Liturgical Renewal and at the same time be shown, as concretely as possible, how missionary worship can be a pastoral factor of primary importance even now, without special permissions from Rome. At the same time, it was kept in mind that the fundamental study and probing into the missionary situation would also bring individual wishes to light which still await the approval of ecclesiastical authority.

The papers of this meeting were of great value, as can be judged even from the list of contents and contributors.[11]

The Eichstätt Study Week (July 21–28) in Germany was the high point of the modern catechetical renewal. Starting with Jungmann's Frohbotschaft in 1936, it led to the German Catechism, the product of fifteen years' collaboration in the catechetical field. The proponents of the new movement returned to the kerygma (that is, the core of Christianity), discarding the scholastic and historical accretions that had robbed the Christian message of its dynamism.

At Eichstätt the kerygmatic movement seemed to reach its peak as hundreds of catechists from all over the world gathered to study the full meaning of the kerygmatic movement.

Its papers have been published in English as *Teaching All Nations*,[12] edited by Johannes Hoffinger. Father Nebreda gives a summary of the main principles of Eichstätt as a guide to catechetical renewal:

1. Basic idea: The catechetical apostolate is a mission imparted by the Church to participate in Christ's proclamation of the good news of salvation. The whole of catechetics is to be inspired and governed by this idea.
2. Aim: The aim of the catechetical apostolate is not knowledge as such, but living faith—man's response to God's call (message).

[11] The English version of these papers was published as *Liturgy and the Missions*, ed. Johannes Hofinger (Collegeville, Minnesota: 1960).

[12] Johannes Hofinger, S.J., ed., *Teaching All Nations* (Freiburg: Herder, 1961).

3. Message: The emphasis is to be on content more than on method. As for content, we should stress the central theme of God's love accomplished in Jesus Christ (dead, risen, and living in his Church), presented as a gospel (good news) oriented to life.

4. Method: Methodology must follow the dynamics of faith: present the religious facts, unfold their religious meaning, and stimulate a personal, vital response to God's call. As such method is a handmaid, but an indispensable one. In all its phases it needs thorough adaptation to those to be catechized.

5. Fourfold presentation of the faith: Genuine catechetics requires the sound blending of a fourfold presentation of the faith: through the Bible, liturgy, Church's *magisterium,* and Christian witness. Systematic teaching is not to be begun before the age of ten or twelve, and even then needs to be biblical and liturgical in orientation.

6. The Catechist: Because the teacher of religion is Christ's spokesman and witness, he is more important than the textbook. He must personally assimilate the message. He must build up his religious life from the message and harmonize it with his professional training.

7. Textbooks: Textbooks are at the service of the teacher and the pupils. Those taking into account the development of present-day theology are a necessity. Outdated texts cannot be modernized by mere modification or revision. Modern catechetics is basically a spiritual, theological, and pastoral renewal, not just a methodological and psychological advancement.[13]

The Bangkok East Asian Study Week (1962) went on from the Eichstätt position and, as we have already seen, brought into clear focus for the first time in the history of catechetics the three stages which normally characterise the journey of an adult to faith: (1) Pre-evangelisation; that is, a stage of preparation for the kerygma which, taking man as he is and where he is, makes a human dialogue possible and awakens in him the sense of God, an indispensable element for opening his heart to the message. (2) Evangelisation or kerygma; that is, the dynamic heralding of the substance of the Christian message, having as its goal personal conversion or initial acceptance of Christ as the Lord. (3) Catechesis

---

[13] A. M. Nebreda, S.J., *Kerygma in Crisis* (Chicago: Loyola University Press, 1965), p. 39.

proper, which leans on the conversion achieved by the previous stages and systematically develops the message. Its goal is to initiate man into Christian life and build within him a Christian personality.

The first Pan African Catechetical Congress took place at Kaligondo Seminary in Uganda from 27th August to 1st September, 1964.

According to the introduction by the editor of the symposium, this was a milestone not only in the history of catechetics in Africa, but in the whole of Catholic mission history. Its great stress was on the Bible. As the editor remarked, "For many portions of the world we have yet really to *translate* the *Word* not into more words, but into flesh and blood." [14]

In this last chapter, as a missionary, I have stressed—perhaps unduly—developments in mission fields. But it is important to realise that very much of what has happened there (especially the publications resulting) has a universal validity so far as principles are concerned. The relation between the Assisi-Rome and the one at Eichstätt illustrates this is considered something precious which has to be shrouded in metaphor and symbol to guard against profanation. These are taught and explained only to people who are worthy and who have shown that they appreciate them.

Two things, therefore, seem to be general characteristics of Javanese initiation, namely, the air of mystery and, as a result of this, the communication in successive phases. These two characteristics—mystification and gradualness of initiation—could be taken over into our Christian initiation, namely in our administration of baptism, insofar as these characteristics are no longer present in it. This could be true especially for the baptism of adults and the catechumenate preceding it. First of all, one could investigate how far both characteristics of Javanese initiation could be built into the instruction that is given during the catechumenate. Some of the doctrines of the Catholic faith can be reached with natural

---

[14] The papers were published as *Katigondo Presenting the Christian Message to Africa*, edited by Robert Ledogar, M.M. (London: Geoffrey Chapman, 1965).

reason or are also known in other religions. Also, with regard to the mysteries there are graduations because they are not all equally simple. There is not space for further examples, but the book *God in Viet-Nam* by Jaques Dournes, which describes how a French missionary, alone among the Jarai tribe on a desolate plateau in Viet-Nam, entered into the life of the people, penetrated their manners, customs, and culture, and brought to what he calls "the sickness of the Jarai religion" (which had grown old, irrelevant, and decadent) "the remedy of an inward renewal of its essential ideas whose meaning we perfected by using them to translate the message of revelation to prevent the Mission suffering from the inconstancy—if not the outright duplicity—of neophytes who had not the patients for conversion, we formed a catechumenate so organised as to help pagans pass from one religious system to another." Of this book and of these efforts, Father Henri de Lubac, S.J., has said:

> The problems arising out of everything he sets out to do admit of no straightforward, once-for-all solutions: there are problems of language and therefore of translation, problems of ritual and therefore of adaptation, problems of religious teaching and therefore of education as a whole, and so on. The whole intellectual activity of the Church in our time must be there to help him solve each as it comes. But it is not a one-way traffic; all that it has gained from present-day theological writing, from the biblical, patristic and liturgical renewals, the work described in these pages is able to give back in enriching the labours of the theologians. It has more to bring to the renewal of theology's life-blood than many an erudite thesis or academic study—valuable though these may be.

In 1966, in Holland, the Dutch Catechism[15] was published. It is evidently meant for more developed minds, and meant to be read, pondered over, and reread.

It forms one whole, "the *Word*" really being translated "not into mere words, but into flesh and blood." There is no series of dogmatic statements and ecclesiastical decisions, or direct or obvious settling of controversial points, but one

---

[15] *De Nieuwe Katechismus, Feloofsverkondiging voor Volwassesen* (*The New Catechism, Religious Doctrine for Adults*) (Hilversum/ Antwerp: Paul Brand).

"narrative" in which people find the doctrine of Christ and of his Church, so that they themselves can conscientiously arrange their lives accordingly. From it one acquires a deep, penetrating knowledge of Catholic doctrine. It is an outline, not a manual of theology. An outline, however, which is a real guide to initiation, in the sense of *making Christians,* not just people who have all the answers, but people who have changed, from being merely ignorant, or merely external Christians, into internally Christ-centred men and women. It is proper *formation* of Christians; yet, once digested, it makes one possess a wealth of information on Christian truth, in the modern setting and adapted to present-day circumstances and changed conditions, fitting the advanced knowledge in the human and biological fields.

It is especially useful for those who give religious education, whether it be instruction of children or of adults. But the intention is that it should wholly penetrate the mind and heart of the reader-instructor; only thus will one be able to fulfil one's task: in one's own way communicating to others this "living faith," bringing them no dry, dogmatic exposé, but a living knowledge of the fulness of Christ's message. Obviously this approach and much of the material will be of great use in other countries and other parts of the world in the task of religious initiation.

What is now clear is that the Church is on the threshold—indeed, has passed over it—of a dynamic revolutionary change in the whole approach to the work of preaching the Gospel and making "converts of all nations." The Vatican Council and the wealth of ideas it has fermented have given a powerful impetus, as well as the official approval of the whole Church, to this movement which resembles a second Pentecost, but at the same time goes back to the first Pentecost for its inspiration and even its methods.